P9-DBT-604

CAPTURED *by* GRACE

DAVID JEREMIAH

with Dr. David Jeremiah

© 2005, 2010 by Turning Point for God
P.O. Box 3838
San Diego, CA 92163
All Rights Reserved

Unless otherwise indicated, Scripture verses quoted are taken from the NEW KING JAMES VERSION.

Printed in the United States of America.

CONTENTS

About
Dr. David Jeremiah
and Turning Point

D r. David Jeremiah is the founder of Turning Point, a ministry committed to providing Christians with sound Bible teaching relevant to today's changing times through radio and television broadcasts, audio series, and books. Dr. Jeremiah's common-sense teaching on topics such as family, prayer, worship, angels, and biblical prophecy forms the foundation of Turning Point.

David and his wife, Donna, reside in El Cajon, California, where he serves as the senior pastor of Shadow Mountain Community Church. David and Donna have four children and ten grandchildren.

In 1982, Dr. Jeremiah brought the same solid teaching to San Diego television that he shares weekly with his congregation. Shortly thereafter, Turning Point expanded its ministry to radio. Dr. Jeremiah's inspiring messages can now be heard worldwide on radio and television, and the Internet.

Because Dr. Jeremiah desires to know his listening audience, he travels nationwide holding ministry rallies and spiritual enrichment conferences that touch the hearts and lives of many people. According to Dr. Jeremiah, "At some point in time, everyone reaches a turning point; and for every person, that moment is unique, an experience to hold onto forever. There's so much changing in today's world that sometimes it's difficult to choose the right path. Turning Point offers people an understanding of God's Word as well as the opportunity to make a difference in their lives."

Dr. Jeremiah has authored numerous books, including *Escape the Coming Night* (Revelation), *The Handwriting on the Wall* (Daniel), *Overcoming Loneliness, Grand Parenting, The Joy of Encouragement, Prayer—The Great Adventure, God in You* (Holy Spirit), *Gifts from God* (Parenting), *Jesus' Final Warning, When Your World Falls Apart, Slaying the Giants in Your Life, My Heart's Desire, Sanctuary, Life Wide Open, Searching for Heaven on Earth, The Secret of the Light, Captured by Grace, Discover Paradise, Grace Givers, Why the Nativity?, Signs of Life, The 12 Ways of Christmas, 1 Minute a Day, What in the World Is Going On?* and *Living With Confidence in a Chaotic World.*

ABOUT THIS STUDY GUIDE

The purpose of this Turning Point study guide is to reinforce Dr. David Jeremiah's dynamic, in-depth teaching and to aid the reader in applying biblical truth to his or her daily life. This study guide is designed to be used in conjunction with Dr. Jeremiah's *Captured by Grace* audio series, but it may also be used by itself for personal or group study.

STRUCTURE OF THE LESSONS

Each lesson is based on one of the messages in the *Captured by Grace* compact disc series and focuses on specific passages in the Bible. Each lesson is composed of the following elements:

• *Outline*

The outline at the beginning of the lesson gives a clear, concise picture of the topic being studied and provides a helpful framework for readers as they listen to Dr. Jeremiah's teaching.

• *Overview*

The overview summarizes Dr. Jeremiah's teaching on the passage being studied in the lesson. Readers should refer to the Scripture passages in their own Bibles as they study the overview.

• *Application*

This section contains a variety of questions designed to help readers dig deeper into the lesson and the Scriptures, and to apply the lesson to their daily lives. For Bible study groups or Sunday school classes, these questions will provide a springboard for group discussion and interaction.

• *Did You Know?*

This section presents a fascinating fact, historical note, or insight that adds a point of interest to the preceding lesson.

USING THIS GUIDE FOR GROUP STUDY

The lessons in this study guide are suitable for Sunday school classes, small-group studies, elective Bible studies, or home Bible study groups. Each person in the group should have his or her own study guide.

When possible, the study guide should be used with the corresponding compact disc series. You may wish to assign the study guide as homework prior to the meeting of the group and then use the meeting time to listen to the CD and discuss the lesson.

FOR CONTINUING STUDY

For a complete listing of Dr. Jeremiah's materials for personal and group study call 1-800-947-1993, go online to www.DavidJeremiah.org, or write to: Turning Point, P.O. Box 3838, San Diego, CA 92163.

Dr. Jeremiah's *Turning Point* program is currently heard or viewed around the world on radio, television, and the Internet in English. *Momento Decisivo,* the Spanish translation of Dr. Jeremiah's messages, can be heard on radio in every Spanish speaking country in the world. The television broadcast is also broadcast by satellite throughout the Middle East with Arabic subtitles.

Contact Turning Point for radio and television program times and stations in your area. Or visit our website at www.DavidJeremiah.org.

CAPTURED BY GRACE

INTRODUCTION

In his book *The Grace Awakening*, Charles Swindoll tells about his last spanking. Feeling rather mature and spirited on the day he became a teenager, he decided to assert his newly won independence. Unfortunately, he picked the wrong person to try to impress: His father.

Chuck was lying on his bed on a muggy, Houston afternoon while outside the open window his father was weeding the garden. "Charles, come out and help me weed the garden," his dad called to him. Chuck replied to the effect that, No, it's my birthday, remember?—or something equally foolish and sassy. He knew better than to disobey or disrespect his father, but his newly minted status as a teen was more than he could suppress. His father was in the house in a flash, spanking Chuck all the way out to the garden where he weeded until past dark.

Later that same evening Chuck's father took him out for a surprise birthday dinner. "He gave me what I deserved earlier," Chuck recalled. "Later he gave me what I did not deserve. The birthday dinner was grace."

Grace is receiving what we do not deserve. Grace is different from mercy in that mercy is *not* receiving what we do deserve. (Chuck didn't receive mercy—he got what he deserved!)

Here's a biblical example: In the Old Testament, David didn't deserve to be made king but, by God's grace, he was. David deserved to be put to death for his sins of adultery and murder but, by God's mercy, he wasn't. He got something he didn't deserve and didn't get something he did deserve. Likewise, we have received by grace what we didn't deserve (salvation) and have been spared what we did deserve (judgment).

This study guide is all about the multifaceted jewel of the grace of God. There is a surprise awaiting some Christians who study grace. They know they are saved by grace, but they didn't know they also live by grace. They know their sins were forgiven by grace, but they didn't know grace also gives them ongoing victory over the power of sin. They know that grace was active in their past when they became a Christian, but they didn't know it was also the basis for their present and future as well.

The Greek word for grace in the New Testament is *charis* which can also be translated as "gift." And that is exactly what grace is: The gift of God. The *New Living Translation* renders the most famous passage on grace this way: "God saved you by His special favor when you believed. And you can't take credit for this; it is a gift from God. Salvation is not a reward for the good things we have done, so none of us can boast about it" (Ephesians 2:8–9).

This gift of grace changes our whole life. Paul wrote to Titus that "the grace of God that brings salvation has appeared [PAST] . . . teaching us that, denying ungodliness [PRESENT] . . . we should . . . [look] for the blessed hope and glorious appearing of our great God and Savior Jesus Christ [FUTURE]" (Titus 2:11–13). Grace saves us and teaches us how to live in the present and future. Without grace there would be no Christian life. The alternative would be for us to earn our way to heaven by living perfect lives— and we know how far that would get us.

Have you been *Captured by Grace*? Perhaps you were when you were saved, but have struggled to live the kind of Christian life you believe is possible. It may be that a deeper understanding of God's grace is what you need. May you find it in this study of God's Word of grace to you.

THE CAPTIVATING PRESENCE OF GRACE

Selected Scriptures

In this lesson we are introduced to the amazing grace of God.

OUTLINE

There is a 200-year-old song that in the last forty years has become a sort of national anthem for the world: "Amazing Grace." How ironic that God would put a hymn extolling His grace on the lips of the whole world. God's grace is His gift to those who do not deserve His forgiveness and love.

  I. **The Melody**

  II. **The Man**

 III. **The Message**

 IV. **Grace and Mercy**

It was two weeks before Thanksgiving, 2004. Victoria Ruvolo was driving her car home on the cold, rainy streets of Long Island, New York, after attending her niece's voice recital. Earlier that evening, six young people had broken into a Nissan and stolen a credit card with which they bought $400 worth of DVDs and video games at a nearby store plus a twenty-pound frozen turkey at a grocery store.

Victoria doesn't remember the Nissan heading toward her on the highway, or the teenager hanging out the window. Nor does she remember the frozen turkey he threw at her car that came crashing through her windshield, knocking her unconscious and smashing every bone in her face, leaving her with significant brain damage. Nearly a month later she heard the explanation for the eight-hour surgery that attempted to reconstruct her caved-in face, the four titanium plates supporting her facial bones, the synthetic film holding her eye in place, the tracheotomy and wired jaw. She heard the explanation but couldn't process it.

The young men were caught and all pleaded guilty except one: Ryan Cushing, the eighteen year-old who had thrown the turkey through her windshield. In January, 2005, he entered a plea of not guilty. Had he gone to trial and been found guilty he could have been sentenced to a maximum of twenty-five years in prison. But in August, 2005, with Victoria still undergoing therapy and treatment from the accident, she and Ryan Cushing met for the first time. On August 15, the young man received a plea bargain sentence of six months in jail and five years of probation, to include psychological therapy and public service. The plea bargain had been at the request of Victoria.

When Ryan and Victoria met for the first time that day in court, she threw her arms around the sobbing youth, stroking his hair, telling him she loved him and forgave him, that she wanted the best for his life. The *New York Times* called the scene a "moment of grace": "Given the opportunity for retribution, Ms. Ruvolo gave and got something better: the dissipation of anger and the restoration of hope, in a gesture as cleansing as the tears washing down her damaged face, and the face of the foolish, miserable boy whose life she single-handedly restored."[1]

To say that was a moment of grace is an understatement. At the very least, it was a display of "amazing grace."

Wherever grace is displayed, it short-circuits our whole system of reasoning; it turns all our suppositions upside down. Grace is unexpected and undeserved and catches us off guard. We think, "Surely there is a part of this story I have not heard." We shake our heads, marvel for a few days or weeks, and eventually return to the routine of our lives.

But there are some people for whom an encounter with grace is a life-changing experience. The apostle Paul, the man who wrote most of the letters in the New Testament, was one such person. He never got over the grace God extended to him. This is obvious as you read Paul's letters. His logical, theological, or practical writing will be moving steadily ahead when all of a sudden he will divert into a parenthetical passage on the greatness of God (Romans 11:33–36). Paul was ready to marvel at the grace of God at anytime.

Of the 155 times the word "grace" appears in the New Testament, 130 of those uses can be attributed to the writings of Paul. Grace is at the heart of his writings. Paul was characterized by a lot of things, but perhaps by nothing more than grace.

There is another man for whom grace was a life-changer, a man who lived many centuries after Paul. His name is John Newton, the author of the famous hymn "Amazing Grace." He was the former slave trader who lived a sinful and blasphemous life before being nearly drowned at sea. He realized God had saved him and repented of his sins, becoming a pastor in Olney, England, for sixteen years. He kept a small plaque over his fireplace with quotations from Deuteronomy 15:15 and Isaiah 43:4: "You shall remember that you were a slave in the land of Egypt, and the Lord your God redeemed you . . . . Since you were precious in My sight, you have been honored, and I have loved you." That plaque helped John Newton remember what God's grace had done for him.

THE MELODY

John Newton wrote "Amazing Grace" in 1773. It was his custom as a pastor to compose hymns to accompany the sermons he preached. And such was the origin of "Amazing Grace." On New Year's Day, 1773, Newton was preaching on 1 Chronicles 17:16–17: "Then King David went in and sat before the LORD; and he said: 'Who am I, O Lord God? And what is my house, that You have brought me this far? And yet this was a small thing in Your sight, O God; and You have also spoken of Your servant's house for a great while to come, and have regarded me according to the rank of a man of high degree, O Lord God.' "

You might wonder what this sermon would have had to do with the grace of God. I have read John Newton's sermon and he preached it like he was David. It was God's grace that chose David to become king of Israel and forgive him for his sins as king, and it was God's grace that gave John Newton the opportunity to be forgiven for all he had done as well. And so John Newton became a preacher of the grace of God.

The great hymn we are so familiar with today took an amazing path over the last 200-plus years. First, there were three additional verses written by John Newton which do not appear in our hymn-books today:

> The Lord has promised good to me,
> His word my hope secures;
> He will my shield and portion be,
> As long as life endures.

> Yes, when this flesh and heart shall fail,
> And mortal life shall cease,
> I shall possess, within the veil,
> A life of joy and peace.

> The earth shall soon dissolve like snow,
> The sun forbear to shine;
> But God, who called me here below,
> Will be forever mine.

In addition, the fourth verse in the current versions of "Amazing Grace" ("When we've been there ten thousand years . . . .") was not written by Newton. The words to this verse were found by Edwin Excell in Harriet Beecher Stowe's anti-slavery novel, *Uncle Tom's Cabin* (1852). Excell took those words and put them with the three verses of "Amazing Grace" that were in use, making up the four-verse hymn we know today.

But that's not all. "Amazing Grace" wasn't always the popular hymn and song it is today. Something happened in 1970 that catapulted it into the mainstream of music. Folk singer Judy Collins recorded an *a cappella* version of the hymn in December, 1970. By January, 1971, it was a number one hit in America and Great Britain, and is now perhaps the best-known hymn in the world—more than 200 years after it was written by the one who had experienced the amazing grace of God.

This hymn has been used in recent Olympic ceremonies, presidential inaugurations, and memorials for the 9–11 terrorist attacks. And with the help of some of my younger, tech-savvy friends, we discovered that there are more than 3,800 versions of "Amazing Grace" available at a major Internet music retailer.

I cite the history of this song and its present-day widespread use to point out one thing: What might be considered the most-loved song in the world is about the amazing grace of God. I think it's pretty amazing that God has made a song about His grace become a sort of "national anthem" for the modern world.

THE MAN

Saint Augustine is credited with saying that God never pours His grace into anything other than empty hands. And John Newton was a man with empty hands. As a result, when he most needed it, he received the grace of God.

John Newton was an only child, born on July 24, 1725, in England. His father, a seaman, was absent during most of John's childhood. His mother, Elizabeth, was a godly woman who gave her son a spiritual upbringing. She invested great effort in teaching him the Scriptures and taking him to a small, Bible-teaching chapel in London at a time when 99 percent of the church attendees went to the Anglican Church, the state church of England.

Sadly, this godly woman died in 1732, just before John turned seven. His father quickly remarried and shuttled his son off to a boarding school at Stratford. At the age of ten, he returned home—and that was the extent of his formal education. By age seventeen, John had replaced the godly training from his mother with a life of rebellion that lasted until age twenty-four. He wrote in his own journal that it was his "delight and habitual practice to be wicked"; that he "neither feared God nor regarded men"; and that he "was a slave to doing wickedness and delighted in sinfulness."

After a short stint in the British Navy, John went AWOL to search for his father, hoping to find a better life. But he was captured, beaten publicly, stripped of his rank, thrown into shackles, and returned to the Navy. He eventually got off the Naval ship onto a ship bound for Africa where he thought he would be free to do whatever he wanted. Unfortunately, things only got worse.

He made it to an island off the west coast of Africa where he lived with a Portuguese slave trader whose wife treated him cruelly—like an animal. But he was so desperate that he "received with thanks and eagerness as the most needy beggar" the scraps of food she gave him. He escaped that situation by building a fire on the shore, trying to signal a passing ship. He was rescued and worked on that ship for a year. Then, in March, 1748, on the ship's return to England, God did a work of grace in John Newton's life that changed him forever—and qualified him to write the hymn we so love today. (More about those events in an upcoming lesson!)

Back in England, John Newton married his childhood sweetheart, Mary Catlett. For ten years he supported his family by working as a surveyor in Liverpool. He had returned to the roots of his faith, was growing as a Christian, and began to wonder if God might want him to become a minister—a preacher of the Word. So he set about studying to prepare himself. Besides the Scriptures, he taught himself Greek, Hebrew, Syriac, Latin, and French.

In 1764, he accepted a call to the pastorate of the Church of England parish in Olney, England, which he served for sixteen years. At age fifty-four he transferred to the much larger St. Mary's church in London where he served another twenty-seven years, preaching his last sermon there when he was eighty-one years old. When asked why he preached so long, he would say, "What? Can the old African blasphemer stop preaching as long as he still has breath?"

The grace that saved John Newton kept him preaching right up to the end.

THE MESSAGE

The melody and the man make for fascinating history, and to much of the world that's all there is to the song. But Christians know there is a message in "Amazing Grace" that is at the heart of its power. I have seen some New Age writers who have tried to adapt words of "Amazing Grace" for their own purposes, saying it refers to a higher consciousness and unity that we have with one another. Judy Collins, the singer who put the song on modern pop charts, said this about the song's meaning: "It's letting go, bottoming out, seeing the light, turning it over, trusting the universe, breathing in, breathing out, going with the flow." Somehow, I don't find all these alternative meanings in John Newton's words.

It is time for Christians to reemphasize John Newton's original message: That God's grace is the only thing powerful enough to save "a wretch like me." The lyrics of this song are all about sinners saved by grace—the same message as the Bible itself.

In the Greek language of the New Testament, the word for grace is *charis* (the "ch" is pronounced like a "k"—"karis"). At its root, *charis* means "gift," and is the same word used to describe the spiritual gifts in the New Testament. You can see that emphasis in our modern word "charismatic." So *charis* became the word for the free gift of God's favor, or God's grace. Someone has said that grace can be spelled J-e-s-u-s, since it was Jesus who was "full of grace and truth," as the apostle John wrote (John 1:14, 17). Ephesians 2:8 says, "For by grace you have been saved through faith, and that not of yourselves; it is the gift of God."

Gifts are not something we receive because we deserve them. Rather, they are received because of the generosity and the initiative of the giver. I have never met a Christian who believed that he deserved the grace of God he received. No one who truly understands grace would believe it was something he had earned and therefore deserved. When I watched the movie, *The Passion of the Christ*, I just kept thinking how I didn't deserve the grace made possible by Christ's suffering in my place. Grace is God's undeserved favor given to those who could never earn it.

Grace is the unsought, undeserved, unconditional love of God. Grace is God pursuing us until He finds us and then preserving us forever afterwards. Grace means more than we could ever put into words because, in essence, grace is who God is. In fact, in 1 Peter we are told that God is "the God of all grace" (1 Peter 5:10). He is the One who gives grace to us that we do not deserve.

GRACE AND MERCY

A good way to understand grace is to compare it with mercy. Because grace and mercy often appear in the same Bible passages, some people think they are synonyms. But they are not. Here is how they differ:

- Mercy is God withholding from us what we truly deserve. (For example, judgment.)
- Grace is God giving to us what we don't deserve. (For example, forgiveness.)

So mercy and grace work together, one protecting us from what we deserve and the other blessing us with what we don't deserve. And grace is more than just forgiveness. Grace is God's forgiveness *through Jesus Christ*. Without God, in His mercy, diverting our judgment onto Jesus Christ, there could be no grace. God's justice was satisfied. We were spared judgment (mercy) so we could be forgiven (grace).

Mercy releases us from the penalty of our sin; grace gives us abundant blessings besides. And that is what God does for all who will accept His free gift of grace in Jesus Christ. Mercy cuts the bonds that bind us to our past; grace sends us into the future with resources for a better life. Mercy removes the filthy rags of our self-righteousness; grace clothes us with the white robes of the righteousness of Christ.

God's grace is truly amazing—and it is yours to receive today!

Note:

1. www.nytimes.com/2005/08/17/opinion/17wed4.html

1. Read Ephesians 2:1–10.

   a. What human spiritual condition do you find in verse 1 that demonstrates what we deserved because of our sin?

   b. Why did we deserve spiritual death? (verses 2–3)

   c. What did God do in spite of what we deserved? (verse 1a)

   d. Is God's making us "alive" an act of grace or of mercy? (verse 4a)

   e. How is our being made alive an act of mercy? (Refer back to the definition of mercy in this lesson if needed.)

   f. Why did God exercise mercy toward us? (verse 4b)

   g. We deserved to remain _____ in our sins, but God _____ us up because of His great _____ with which He _____ us.

   h. By what were we saved from death? (verse 8a)

   i. What was the source of our faith? (verse 8b)

j. What are we unable to do, having been saved by grace? (verse 9)

k. What is the ultimate purpose for our having been saved by grace? (verse 10)

l. What will we spend the "ages to come" learning more about? (verse 7)

2. How might you exercise mercy toward one of your children?

   a. After the exercise of mercy, how might you show them grace?

   b. Is it possible to show mercy without grace? Are they that separate? Or does grace always follow mercy?

   c. Can you cite a time when you were shown mercy by another person? Grace? What impact did it have on your future behavior?

3. What was the evidence of "great grace" that was upon the apostles? (Acts 4:33)

   a. In what way is grace sovereign in the affairs of man and God? (Romans 5:21)

b. How would you define the effects of the riches of God's grace? (Ephesians 1:7)

c. What was the evidence of the grace of God in the church at Corinth? (2 Corinthians 9:13–14)

d. How are spiritual gifts an evidence of the "manifold grace of God?" (1 Peter 4:10)

e. How is grace sufficient for those who suffer? (2 Corinthians 12:9)

f. What does it mean for grace to abound more than sin? (Romans 5:20)

g. How was the gift of the grace of God manifested? (Romans 5:15)

h. Why is grace glorious? (Ephesians 1:5–6)

4. Read Romans 6:23.

   a. How would you describe the difference between wages and a gift?

   b. _____ are something we earn; a _____ is something we receive.

   c. Have you sinned? (Romans 3:23)

   d. What are the wages of sin? What did you "earn" by your sin?

   e. What is the gift God makes available to you?

DID YOU KNOW?

In the eighteenth century, the words to hymns were written and then matched with a tune that fit the words. That's what happened with "Amazing Grace." The words to this famous hymn were paired with twenty different tunes before the melody we now know was settled upon. It is a melody called "New Britain," and was combined with John Newton's words in 1829, long after the words were written in 1773. And the hymn was not originally called "Amazing Grace." The original name was "Faith's Review and Expectation."

THE COMPASSIONATE PLAN OF GRACE

Romans 3:9–25

*In this lesson we learn how the grace of God
is the answer to the sin of man.*

OUTLINE

Some people don't believe they've sinned, and others think they've sinned too much to ever be saved. Once we acknowledge we've sinned, the next step is to realize that God's redemption is free. We can't earn it or work for it. If we could, it wouldn't be free—and wouldn't be by grace.

I. **Prelude to Grace**

II. **Principles of Grace**
   A. Grace—Apart From Works
   B. Grace—Accepted by Faith
   C. Grace—Available to All Who Believe
   D. Grace—Attained by Justification
   E. Grace—Awarded Freely
   F. Grace—Acquired Through Redemption
   G. Grace—Accomplished Through Propitiation

John Newton wrote in his now-famous song that grace had saved a "wretch" like him. That word is so offensive to our modern sensibilities that many people replace it with another, less negative, term when they sing "Amazing Grace."

But Newton knew from his own experience that he was a wretch when God saved him. Indeed, all men are wretches in that they are lost in sin. That is the biblical truth. But Newton knew that truth first-hand. A dictionary definition of "wretch" includes these words: "a miserable person . . . profoundly unhappy . . . sunk in vice or degradation . . . a vile person." John Newton would have said, "That was me, to the letter!"

On one of his lonely stints at sea, Newton was so depressed and full of anger that he considered taking his life; was so angry at his captain he considered killing him as well! In a letter he wrote in 1754 he said that, before he reached the age of twenty, he was never in another person's company more than an hour "without attempting to corrupt them." He once said of himself, "My daily life was a course of the most terrible blasphemy and profaneness. I don't believe that I have ever since met so daring a blasphemer as myself . . . . I not only sinned with a high hand myself but made it my study to tempt and seduce others upon every occasion."

A contemporary theologian by the name of Cornelius Plantinga, who is now the president of Calvin College, has written a very challenging book called *It's Not Supposed to Be This Way: A Breviary of Sin*. In his book, he warns us against any consideration of the grace of God that does not first contemplate the sinfulness of man. Here is a brief paragraph from what he wrote.

> To speak of grace without sin is . . . to trivialize the cross of Jesus Christ . . . and therefore to cheapen the grace of God that always comes to us with blood on it. What had we thought the ripping and the writhing on Golgotha were all about? To speak of grace without looking squarely at these realities, without painfully honest acknowledgment of our own sin and its effects, is to shrink grace to a mere embellishment of the music of creation, to shrink it down to a mere grace note. In short, for the Christian church (even in its recently popular seeker services) to ignore, euphemize or otherwise mute the lethal reality of sin is to cut the nerve of the Gospel. For the sober truth is that

without...sin, the gospel of grace becomes impertinent, unnecessary, and finally uninteresting.[1]

John Newton eventually found great hope in the apostle Paul's words that he was, among sinners, "chief" (1 Timothy 1:15). Since Paul had attacked and persecuted Christians, yet had been saved by grace, he thought there must be hope for him as well. It was John Newton's recognition of sin in his own life that awakened him to the grace of God.

PRELUDE TO GRACE (ROMANS 3:10–20)

The prelude to grace is an understanding that we need grace, and we only understand that we need grace when we see our own sin.

In his bold and helpful book, *Why Sin Matters*, Mark R. McMinn writes:

> Recognizing our sin is the prelude to grace. Sin is not a popular word. Perhaps it evokes images of angry fundamentalist preachers who seem more intent on condemning and judging than searching for forgiveness and grace. Maybe the word has been used to manipulate and coerce you to behave more like someone wants you to behave. Or possibly the word sin has been the topic of lighthearted joking and has lost its gravity.[2]

Many pastors today don't like to talk about sin from the pulpit for fear people will leave their service depressed. That would be the equivalent of going to the doctor and having him discover you have cancer, but giving you this report: "I found a couple of problems, but I don't want to ruin your day by talking about those. On the positive side, I can report that you have a strong pulse and your blood pressure is fine."

Would you go back to see a doctor who treated you that way? Not likely. Until we are told we have a sickness called sin, we'll never appropriate the medicine called grace. Our modern world spends most of its time trying to cover up the root issue of many human problems, which is sin. We would rather blame our problems on anything else than face up to them ourselves. Why would I need God's grace if I am convinced I don't have any problems?

The apostle Paul did not attempt to ignore sin in his life. The older he got, the more realistically he dealt with it. In 1 Corinthians 15:9, he called himself the "least of the apostles." In Ephesians 3:8 he said he was "less than the least of all the saints." And in 1 Timothy 1:15, he said he was the chief of sinners—from the least of the apostles to the chief of sinners over his lifetime. The longer he lived, the more Paul's eyes were opened to his need for the grace of God. It's not that he sinned more; indeed, I'm sure he sinned less. He just became more and more aware of his own sinful nature and how much he needed the grace of God.

In Romans 3:10–18 Paul strung together a series of quotes from the Old Testament that was sufficient to cover every person alive—there is no one who is not a sinner in need of the grace of God:

As it is written:

There is none righteous, no, not one;
There is none who understands;
There is none who seeks after God.
They have all turned aside;
They have together become unprofitable;
There is none who does good, no, not one.
Their throat is an open tomb;
With their tongues they have practiced deceit;
The poison of asps is under their lips;
Whose mouth is full of cursing and bitterness.
Their feet are swift to shed blood;
Destruction and misery are in their ways;
And the way of peace they have not known.
There is no fear of God before their eyes.

Notice how often Paul uses the words "all" and "none" (or "not one"). Paul makes it clear that there is not a single person who has hope of being righteous apart from God.

The Puritan theologians had it right when they wrote that man is "totally depraved." That doesn't mean we are as bad as we could be. It means that depravity extends to every part of our being; that there is not one part of us that is untainted by sin. Chuck Swindoll put it this way:

If depravity were blue, we'd be blue all over. Cut us anywhere and we'll bleed blue. Cut our minds and you'll find blue thoughts. Cut our vision and there are blue images full of greed and lust. Cut into our hearts and there are blue emotions of hatred, revenge and lust. Cut into our wills and you'll find deep blue decisions and responses.[3]

Even in our best moments, we have the potential to lapse into sin; when serving others, we can find ourselves doing it for selfish or self-centered reasons. To skip over sin in the presentation of the biblical gospel is to miss the need for grace. That's why Paul called it the "gospel of the grace of God" (Acts 20:24). We cannot receive the good news of grace until we've dealt with the bad news of sin.

The very idea of a Savior necessitates the reality of sin. What does a Savior save us from if not from sin? Many today would have Jesus be a Savior from poor self-esteem, from discouragement, or from oppressive ideologies. Those may get dealt with along the way, but that is not the first thing Jesus saves us from. The first thing we need is to be saved from the condemnation and power of sin.

PRINCIPLES OF GRACE (ROMANS 3:21–25)

Now that we have the diagnosis, it's time to consider the cure: The grace of God. Paul outlines seven components of grace in these five verses, which the great commentator Donald Grey Barnhouse said were the greatest in all the Bible—the heart of the Gospel.[4]

When I was diagnosed with cancer, I was so relieved to find out it was a "curable" kind. I know it can be devastating for those who discover no cure yet exists for the disease they have contracted. But what a great encouragement to know that there is a cure for the disease of sin! And that cure is the grace of God.

Grace—Apart From Works (Verse 21)

As a young man, I heard a preacher say that getting to heaven was like being in a boat with two oars: One oar of works and one of grace. When I got older and understood the Bible better, I realized you'd be going around in a circle for eternity because one of those oars doesn't work—the oar of works. If works could get us to heaven, even part of the way there, God would not have sent His Son to die on a cross for us—to do it all. The grace of God is revealed to us totally apart from the works of the Law.

This is what sets Christianity apart from all the world's religions. Christianity is a religion of divine accomplishment; the rest are religions of human achievement. Second Timothy 1:9 tells us God has "saved us . . . not according to our works, but according to His own purpose and grace " (see also Titus 3:5).

Grace—Accepted by Faith (Verse 22)

Paul says we receive the righteousness of God through faith in Jesus Christ. Someone said that faith is the channel through which the grace of God comes to us—and I agree.

Charles Haddon Spurgeon said, "Faith is believing that Christ is what He is said to be, and that He will do what He has promised to do, and then to expect this of Him."[5] Faith is believing what God says about righteousness through Christ and acting upon it.

Grace—Available to All Who Believe (Verses 22–23)

Some people believe they are not candidates for the grace of God, that they have sinned beyond what God's grace can cover. But there is no difference in the amount of sin in different people's lives. Your life is like a cup of water. It doesn't matter whether you put a speck, a thimbleful, or a tablespoon full of dirt in it—any dirt at all makes the water undrinkable. You can be a rabid sinner or an occasional sinner—it makes no difference as far as God's grace is concerned. All are lost—there is none righteous.

That's why grace is available to all, because all are sinners in God's sight. Grace is available to all who believe in Christ (John 14:6).

Grace—Attained by Justification (Verse 24)

This verse contains an important theological word that needs defining: justified. My father used to say, when I was growing up, that "justified" means "Just-as-if-I'd never sinned." That's a pretty good definition. The problem with it is, we really did sin!

When a president of the United States pardons someone, all he does is make the person not accountable for their crime or misdeed. The president can pardon, but he can't justify. Justification means restoring you to the status you had before you sinned—making it as if you'd never sinned. That's what God does through Christ. He sees us as if we had never sinned (though we have) because Christ took our sins upon himself. And He does that by His grace.

Grace—Awarded Freely (Verse 24)

We are justified "freely by His grace." In the Latin version of the New Testament, the word "freely" is translated into *gratis*. If you've ever been offered something *gratis*, you know it means that it's free. God's grace is *gratis*—"being justified freely by His grace."

We have a hard time with this in our culture because we've been taught that you have to work hard for everything you get. I've talked to many successful businessmen through the years who have a hard time with the idea of not "paying their own way" to heaven. But you can't pay for something that's free. If you had to work for grace, it wouldn't be grace—because grace is free, unmerited favor from God. We have to receive it freely or not at all.

Grace—Acquired Through Redemption
(Verse 24)

With "redemption," Paul draws a word from the economic vocabulary of his day—a term used to describe the purchase of slaves in the marketplace in New Testament times. Even in the sad history of our own country—the slave trade in which John Newton was involved—slaves would be brought into a marketplace like cattle. Those who were there to purchase slaves for their farms or other work settings would purchase them out of the marketplace— they would redeem them. Their shackles would be removed and the slaves would go home with their new owner.

Paul uses the word "redemption" to describe what happens to us when we freely receive the grace of God. Our shackles are re-moved, we are purchased out of the marketplace of sin, and God becomes our new owner.

I have stood in the marketplace of Charleston, South Carolina, which used to be an entry port for slaves into this country from Africa. It was sickening and shameful to stand in a place where human beings were once treated like property. But it also gave me a fitting picture of what God has done for me by grace—redeeming me from the marketplace of sin.

Grace—Accomplished Through Propitiation
(Verse 25)

Propitiation is a hard word, but a biblical one—and a very important one. It comes from the Old Testament—the word for the lid, or "mercy seat," on the ark of the covenant. The ark sat in the Holy of Holies in the tabernacle, and later the temple, and contained the tablets containing the Law received by Moses on Mt. Sinai. There were two cherubim (angels), one on each end of the ark, whose wings stretched over the lid of the ark. God dwelt between the cherubim, hovering over the ark, over the Law He had given Israel—the Law they had broken by their sin. Once a year, on the Day of Atonement, the High Priest would bring the blood of a sacrifice in and pour it over the top of the ark, over the mercy seat. Propitiation, in Greek, came to mean "satisfaction"—God was satisfied with the shed blood that covered the lid of the ark, and thereby covered the broken Law within. When God looked down from above the ark, He did not see the broken Law; rather He saw the shed blood of the sacrifice, and was propitiated, or satisfied.

If you think you have committed too many sins to be forgiven, to be made righteous, to receive the grace of God, remember the mercy seat of the ark of the covenant. God has been propitiated by Christ's blood. If God is satisfied that the blood of Christ is sufficient to cover all your sins, you should be satisfied, too—and receive His grace as freely as it has been offered to you.

Notes:

1. Cornelius Plantinga, Jr., *Not the Way It's Supposed to Be: A Breviary of Sin* (Grand Rapids: William B. Eerdmans, 1995), 199.

2. Mark R. McMinn, *Why Sin Matters* (Wheaton: Tyndale, 2004), 14.

3. Charles R. Swindoll, *Growing Deep in the Christian Life* (Portland: Multnomah Press, 1986), 207.

4. Donald Grey Barnhouse, *God's Remedy, God's River – Romans-Vol. II* (Grand Rapids: William B. Eerdmans, 1953), 5–6.

5. Charles Haddon Spurgeon, *All of Grace* (Chicago: Moody Press), 47.

1. Read Romans 3:10–18.

   a. How many naturally righteous people have ever lived? (verse 10)

   b. How many have natural understanding of God? (verse 11a)

   c. How many people, on their own, seek after God to know Him? (verse 11b)

   d. What do people naturally do when they encounter God? (verse 12a)

   e. What does it mean that people "together become unprofitable?" (verse 12b)

   f. What comes out of the throat of a person naturally? (verses 13–14)

   g. What characteristic is described in verses 15–17?

   h. How much do they fear God? (verse 18)

i. Every non-Christian is not as bad as some of the descriptions Paul uses. So what is Paul saying? Is he speaking literally? Figuratively? What's his point?

j. In what way(s) does Paul's description of the natural man describe you before you came to know Christ?

k. If absolutely no one is good in God's sight, what was necessary in order for man to get to heaven? (Romans 3:24)

l. How does the natural man gain a desire to have faith in Christ? (Ephesians 2:8)

2. Read the account of Paul's conversion in Acts 9:1–18.

a. How much of Paul's initiative was involved in his transformation?

b. How much was God's initiative?

c. Paul was on his way to persecute Christians when he was saved. How was Paul an example of the persons he later wrote about in Romans 3:10–18?

d. How is Paul's conversion an example of salvation being wholly from God?

3. Read 1 Timothy 1:13–15.

a. How does Paul describe himself before he knew Christ? (verse 13a)

b. Why did God show mercy to Paul? (verse 13b)

c. How does Luke 23:34 parallel Paul's words in verse 13b?

d. Given Paul's background, why do you think he makes a point of saying God's grace was "exceedingly abundant?" (verse 14a)

e. What else did Paul receive besides grace? (verse 14b)

f. If Paul was the "chief" of sinners, yet was saved, what is he saying to the rest of us?

4. If we were not called to salvation on the basis of our works, what was the basis of our calling? (2 Timothy 1:9)

   a. If our works were not the basis of our salvation, what was? (Titus 3:5)

   b. How comfortable are you with having not earned even a tiny part of your salvation—receiving it all freely by grace?

   c. How does this affect your relationship with other people—whether they need to earn your forgiveness or not?

5. What do you appreciate most about the "freeness" of grace?

DID YOU KNOW?

The New Testament uses the word "propitiation" four times: Romans 3:25; Hebrews 2:17; 1 John 2:2; 1 John 4:10. Not all translations include Hebrews 2:17 in this list. Some translations use the word "expiation" in that verse; others use "atoning sacrifice." Propitiation and expiation are not synonyms. Propitiation is something done to another. Christ propitiated God in that He satisfied God's judgment against sin. Expiation is something done to crimes or violations of the law—it means to cleanse or remove. So Christ propitiated God and expiated our sins. Both were acts of grace made possible by the shed blood of Christ on our behalf.

THE CONVERTING POWER OF GRACE

Luke 15:11–32

*In this lesson we discover the power of grace
in seeking and saving the lost.*

OUTLINE

Many people today herald Jesus as a person who would associate with the lowly and needy in any society—and He was. But He sought them not for companionship but to save them! Their condition made them aware of their need—a prerequisite for receiving the grace of God.

I. **Humiliation of the Father**

II. **Separation From the Father**

III. **Manipulation of the Father**

IV. **Reconciliation With the Father**

V. **Celebration of the Father**

VI. **Condemnation of the Father**

VII. **Insights**
- A. The Older Brother Was a Son Who Was Living Like a Servant
- B. The Older Brother Was a Sinner Who Thought He Was a Saint

One of the most well-known lines in "Amazing Grace" says, "I once was lost but now am found, was blind but now I see." By John Newton's own admission, he took the first part of the line from the words of the father in the Scripture passage we will consider in this lesson: The story of the prodigal son. The father said of his son who returned home, he "was lost and is found" (Luke 15:32).

Luke 15 has what seem to be three separate parables—a lost sheep, a lost coin, and a lost son. But I believe they are three parts of one parable, all dealing with the same theme: God's heart for the lost. In the parable of the prodigal son, the father, representing God, is the central character. He is mentioned twelve times in the story, beginning with his humiliation in verses 11–12.

THE HUMILIATION OF THE FATHER (VERSES 11–12)

The story opens with the younger son declaring his intention to move out from under his father's authority and demanding his rightful inheritance. Jewish law at the time stipulated that, if there were two sons, the older son receive two-thirds of the inheritance and the younger, one-third. The younger son's request was a terrible insult to the father. He was basically saying, "I want you dead" since the inheritance normally was received only after the death of the father.

The father would have been justified under Jewish law to slap his son across the face and kick him out of his home. Instead, the father humbly granted his son's request. Based on indications in the story (there was livestock, servants, property), the father was likely wealthy and well-respected in the community, making the whole situation even more embarrassing. To accomplish his son's wish, the father had to sell part of his property in order to come up with the money to give his son—highly unusual in the Jewish culture. Normally the property would be sold and the value distributed after the father's death. This selfish son brought great shame upon his father's family and name.

But there is even more going on here from a Jewish cultural perspective: If a Jewish boy left his home with his inheritance and then lost that money while living among the Gentiles, he would no longer be welcome in his home or his village. If he returned after having done such a thing, he would be subject to a "cutting off" ceremony; he would be publicly "cut off" from his family and community. This is somewhat like the Amish shunning ritual; but with the Amish, the shunned person could at least have a place to live with his family. In the Jewish ceremony, the young person would be completely cut off and banned from living among friends and family. He lost all rights to any future benefit from the family.[1]

I believe God's grace has room for us to make foolish mistakes; He doesn't always stop us when we head out the door. God sometimes allows us to reject His own love so we can see for ourselves how much we need Him after the fact.

John Newton had an experience like that. Newton turned his back on his spiritual upbringing and the Lord, and ended up in Africa. When he finally "came to his senses" (Luke 15:17) he returned home to his heavenly Father's house and was received by grace.

SEPARATION FROM THE FATHER
(VERSES 13–16)

The Prodigal Son changed his inheritance into cash that he could carry in his pocket and "journeyed to a far country." As well as being a geographical indicator, "a far country" symbolizes a departure for this boy from his spiritual roots and heritage. He is not only leaving his father but the God of his father.

We have two indications in Luke 15 as to what the boy spent his money on: "prodigal living" (verse 13) and "harlots" (verse 30), assuming the older brother's information was accurate. "Harlots" may have been included in the previous "prodigal living" term. The son probably used his cash, throwing parties and acting like a big spender. As is usually true when that happens, when the money was gone, so were his "friends."

When he ran out of money, a famine came to the land and the entire economy suffered. He had no money, no food, and no job. He hit rock bottom, something that God sometimes allows us to do. But he wasn't yet at the very bottom.

He probably thought, I'll hire myself out to a local farmer, save my money, return home, repay my father's inheritance, and buy my way back into the family. So he joins himself to a farmer, probably a Gentile farmer given that he was away from Israel. So now this young Jewish man has hired himself out as a common laborer to a Gentile—something shameful in his culture—and is sent out to slop the hogs. This was definitely not a kosher job. No self-respecting

Jew would have hired himself out to care for unclean animals like hogs.

This turned out to be a dead-end job. He would never earn enough money to repay his father. He was having to eat the same food the hogs were eating! This was the rock bottom.

MANIPULATION OF THE FATHER (VERSES 17–19)

Jesus says something about the boy in this story that tells us he was now at a turning point in his life: "he came to himself." Some Bible versions say it this way: "he came to his senses," which is a good way of putting it. Sometimes this passage is preached this way: "The young man finally came to himself, fell down on his knees and repented before God."

But does he? Is there anything in this passage to indicate he was sorry for what he had done? Does he acknowledge his rebellion and breaking the heart of his father and humiliating his family before the whole community? If it's there, I can't find it.

Instead of repenting, I think he was just trying to figure out how to get out of the mess he had created for himself. Plan A had been to go to work for a Gentile farmer slopping the hogs—but he didn't even get money for his work (verse 16)! He wasn't going to be able to buy his way back into the family. So he needed a Plan B.

The next plan was to go home, hire himself out as a day laborer on his father's farm, and work until he could repay the money and get reinstated in the family. He wanted to try to fix things to make them like they had never happened—become his father's son again. Still no repentance is evident—he's just trying to figure out how to survive.

The speech he outlined for himself to make to his father (verses 18–19) seems a bit contrived to me; less than genuine; manipulative. He talks about saying "I have sinned against heaven and before you" to his father. But remember to whom Jesus is telling this story: the Pharisees and scribes (verse 2). They knew that these words were first formed in the mouth of the Egyptian Pharaoh who was trying to act repentant so Moses would stop bringing plagues on his land (Exodus 10:16).[2] Pharaoh didn't mean it—he was trying to manipulate Moses, and the Pharisees would have known that. And the young man didn't mean it either at this point in the story. He was planning to use the words for effect only to manipulate his father.

This young man has not yet responded to the grace of God. He's still living for himself; still trying to work his way back into the good graces of his father; still operating in the flesh; still trying to save himself.

RECONCILIATION WITH THE FATHER (VERSES 20–21)

This is a moving scene, to say the least. From a distance, the father recognizes the walk of his son. He was no doubt dressed in rags, unwashed, bearded, hair a mess. Yet the father saw something that told him his son had come home. I can imagine that Jesus' intent is to suggest that the father went to a vantage point outside the city and looked far down the road every day for any sign of his lost son.

The Greek text is interesting here—it emphasizes the words "a great way off," and says the father (literally) raced to meet his son, something no self-respecting Jewish father would ever have done. He would have had to pull up the hem of his robes, exposing his legs and feet in order to run down the road. He was taking upon himself—again—the shame and humiliation his son deserved.

Note: The father does not run to embrace the son as a response to the son's repentance. Instead, the father makes the first move of grace by running to an unrepentant son and showering him with kisses and love. Only then does the son make an apparent heartfelt confession as a result of the grace shown by the father.

In all three stories in Luke 15, this is the pattern. The object lost— a sheep, a coin, a son—is searched for by another. It looks like the son is the hero because he initiated the move to come home. But remember why he was doing it—not because he was sorry, but because he wanted shelter. It is the father who was searching daily for his son and ran to "find" him when he caught a glimpse of him from far away. It is in response to the father that the son realizes what he has done and expresses genuine sorrow in response to his father's searching love.

CELEBRATION OF THE FATHER (VERSES 22–24)

When the father ran to the edge of the village to meet his son, his servants ran with him. He sends for the "best robe"—that would be the father's own robe—to put on his son. It doesn't say if they cleaned the son up first, but the father didn't care. He ordered that the finest robe in the house be brought for him to wear to the banquet the father had in mind.

Next, he ordered a servant to fetch "a ring"—but this wasn't just any ring. This was the family's signet ring, like those we've seen that are pressed into clay or soft wax to seal a document. The father is saying to the son by giving this ring, "You can now represent the family and conduct business in the family name."

To a third servant he issues an order to bring sandals for the boy's feet. In that day, generally speaking, servants went barefooted and members of the family wore sandals. The father wanted it to be apparent to all that this was his son, not a household servant, whom he was welcoming home.

Next is the direction to prepare a fatted calf for a celebratory banquet. (Had the father been fattening this calf up for months in anticipation of the son's return?) This banquet is an earthly version of the joy in heaven when one sinner repents (verses 7, 10).

CONDEMNATION OF THE FATHER
(VERSES 25–32)

Things are going well with the story up to this point—but then the older brother comes in from the field and discovers a celebration in progress. And he is not happy when he discovers the reason. The text says, "he was angry and would not go in." You would think he would have been excited at his brother's change of heart, but he was not. Even when his father pleaded with him to join in the celebration, he would not.

The older brother justified his attitude by reciting his own history of faithfulness in serving the father and never being rewarded for it. He couldn't understand why the one who had lived shamefully should be celebrated.

INSIGHTS

The Older Brother Was a Son
Who Was Living Like a Servant

The older brother saw himself as more of a servant than a son—one who had faithfully carried out the father's commands all his life, but never been rewarded for it. But there is something important to notice in this story regarding the older brother.

When the younger brother came to the father and asked for his inheritance, verse 12 says the father "divided to them his livelihood."

Note—not "to him" (the younger brother), but "to them" (both the brothers). The father liquidated everything and divided his inheritance between both the boys. So whatever is left of the property and the livestock now belongs, not to the father, but to the older brother! Some was liquidated to be able to give money to the younger son, but the older son took his inheritance in the form of the family business. No wonder the father said, "all that I have is yours."

The older brother had been given plenty! But he was so bitter over what the younger brother had done that he refused to even call him "my brother"—he refers to him as "this son of yours" (verse 30).

The Older Brother Was a Sinner Who Thought He Was a Saint

Not only was the older brother a son who was acting like a servant, he was a sinner who thought he was a saint.

Jesus said in the story of the lost sheep that there is more rejoicing in heaven over one sinner who repents than for ninety-nine who don't, or think they don't need to. He was obviously talking about the Pharisees, and he was talking about the older brother in this story. He didn't think he needed to repent of anything: "I never transgressed your commandment at any time" (verse 29). We know this was not true! There has never been a child, except Jesus, who didn't disobey his father's commands at some point. The truth was, the older brother was proud and smug in his self-righteousness. He, like the Pharisees, refused to go into the party and celebrate with a sinner like his younger brother.

Why do you think Jesus told this story in the first place? The answer is found in the first verses of Luke 15. The Pharisees and scribes were complaining because Jesus associated with sinners and even ate with them. But Jesus, in essence, told them three stories to illustrate the fact that He not only ate with sinners, He chased after them like someone would a lost sheep, a lost coin, or a lost son. His mission was to "seek and to save that which was lost" (Luke 19:10). His whole purpose was to do exactly what they were accusing him of—reach out to sinners with the grace of God.

The story of the prodigal son illustrates two "kinds" of sinners in need of grace. The older brother was prideful and self-righteous, and the younger brother was outwardly sinful in his immoral and shameful actions. Both need to be saved. The one representing the

Pharisees—the older brother—was not saved as far as we know, which is a strong warning for us about religious pride.

Have you responded to the grace of God? Regardless of the "kind" of sinner you are, there is only one solution—receive the grace of God in Christ today. If you don't know Christ, you are the lost sheep, the lost coin, and the lost son or daughter He came to seek and save.

Notes:

1. Kenneth E. Bailey, *The Cross & the Prodigal* (Downer's Grove: InterVarsity Press, 2005), 52–53.

2. Kenneth E. Bailey, "The *Pursuing Father*" *Christianity Today*, October 26, 1998, and *www.ctlibrary.com/1778*.

APPLICATION

1. Read Luke 19:1–10.

   a. What was Zacchaeus' occupation? (verse 2)

   b. In whose company were tax collectors usually grouped by the Jewish leaders? (see Matthew 9:11; 21:31)

   c. Why were tax collectors so despised by the Jews? (verse 8b)

   d. If tax collectors were despised, how much more was Zacchaeus? (Note the word "chief" in verse 2, and his resulting financial status.)

   e. How did the people refer to Zacchaeus? (verse 7)

   f. What evidence do you find that he was prepared for the grace of God? (verse 4)

   g. Should curiosity be downplayed? How does God use curiosity as an opening for changing a life? Describe a person you know who became a Christian as a result of "curiosity" about Jesus.

h. What did the people think about Jesus' willingness to associate with Zacchaeus? (verse 7)

i. In short, what explanation does Jesus offer about His willingness to associate with known sinners? (verse 10)

j. How does Mark 2:17 (read 2:15–17 for context) amplify Jesus' words to Zacchaeus?

k. Jesus refers to "the righteous" in Mark 2:17. Is He talking about "righteous" or "self-righteous?" (see Romans 3:10)

l. What good does it do for a doctor to give medicine to a person who does not believe he is sick? What will the person do with the medicine?

m. When you first heard the Gospel, did you believe you were "sick" or "well?" If "well," what changed your mind? How did you come to see your true spiritual condition before God?

2. Read Luke 18:9–14.

   a. To whom was this parable addressed? (verse 1)

   b. What was the "righteousness status" of the two men who went to pray at the temple, given their vocations? Why were both in need of grace? (verse 10)

   c. How did the Pharisee evaluate himself? (verses 11–12)

   d. How did the tax collector evaluate himself? (verse 13)

   e. How did Jesus evaluate them both? (verse 14)

   f. Fill in the blanks in Jesus' statement: "Everyone who _____ himself will be _____, and he who _____ himself will be _____." (verse 14)

g. Comparing this parable with the parable of the prodigal son, fill in the following:

The Pharisee was like the _____ brother.

The tax collector was like the _____ brother.

h. In both parables, what is the message about self-righteousness and the ability to receive grace from God?

3. Has the grace of God been extended to you? How do you know? What evidence is there to indicate your response?

DID YOU KNOW?

The Greek word for "coins" in Luke 15:8 is *drachme*, or drachma. The drachma was a Greek silver coin, roughly equivalent to the Roman denarius, each worth about a day's wages. (See Matthew 20:2 where laborers were paid a denarius for a day's work in the vineyard.) The woman in Jesus' parable about the lost coin had ten silver drachmas, or about ten days' worth of money, or a third of a month's wages. By losing one of those silver coins, she lost the equivalent of one-thirtieth of a month's wages. To judge the significance of that loss to your own finances, subtract 3.33 percent (1/30th) from your monthly salary.

THE CLEAR PERSPECTIVE OF GRACE

Romans 2:1–16

In this lesson we see that grace is what covers us when our unrighteousness is exposed.

OUTLINE

Human beings are capable of living comfortably with double standards. We hold others to higher values than we hold ourselves; we fail to live out the exhortations we give to others. And God sees it all. Our unrighteousness is so pervasive that the grace of God is our only hope.

  I. **God's Judgment Is According to Reality**

 II. **God's Judgment Is According to Integrity**

III. **God's Judgment Is According to Opportunity**

 IV. **God's Judgment Is According to Morality**

  V. **God's Judgment Is According to Impartiality**

 VI. **God's Judgment Is According to Certainty**

In our study of the grace of God, we are using as a backdrop the greatest hymn about grace ever written, "Amazing Grace," written by John Newton in 1773. In this lesson Newton's famous line, "I once was blind, but now I see," is the backdrop for our study.

As often happens to historical events, the story of John Newton has been truncated through the years into a number of key events: He rebelled as a youth, ran away to Africa, found passage on a vessel used for transporting slaves from Africa, cried out to God in a storm on the high seas, was converted, returned to England, became a pastor, and wrote "Amazing Grace." While that makes for a neat story, the truth is a bit different.

After being saved from the terrible storm while on the slave vessel, crying out to God for mercy, and returning to England, his spiritual eyes were indeed opened—but not completely. Though he had become a Christian, after returning to Liverpool, he promptly set sail again back to Africa where he went from village to village purchasing human beings and transporting them as cargo in the slave trade. Sailing across the Atlantic, he studied his Latin Bible in his warm and dry quarters while 200 Africans were crammed into the hold below, living in squalor. After selling his human cargo in Charleston, South Carolina, into a life of hopeless oppression, he attended church and took leisurely strolls around Charleston.

He would continue this life for ten more years, without understanding that slavery and abuse of human beings was a sin. It was such a large part of the culture of his era that neither he nor most of his Christian contemporaries thought it was wrong. It was only many years after his conversion that Newton could write, "I once was blind, but now I see." And I believe a good part of the blindness he refers to is his blindness to his own sin of slave-trading in addition to his earlier rebellion toward God.

After Newton left the slave trade and matured as a Christian, he experienced great remorse over his former business. In 1788 he published a 10,000 word essay, *Thoughts Upon the African Slave Trade*, in which he apologized, and denounced slavery for the sin that it was. He said it was iniquitous, cruel, oppressive, destructive, disgraceful, unlawful, and wrong. And he spent the rest of his life, once his eyes were opened to what he had done, trying to help men like England's William Wilberforce abolish slavery.

At the end of his life, John Newton said to one of his friends, "My memory is nearly gone; but I remember two things: That I am a great sinner, and that Christ is a great Savior." And the same is true for us. As the distance grows between our sinful past and the present, the memory of the details of our sin fades. But we never forget this fact: We are great sinners, and Christ is a great Savior.

We wonder today how Newton could have continued doing what he did. We might ask the same thing of ourselves: Why didn't we stop sinning when we came to know Christ? Someone has written that part of our "mess" is that we don't know just how big a mess we are. Another way of saying it is that deceived people don't know they're deceived. Because most Christians have never committed a felony, abused children, or been hopelessly addicted to drugs or alcohol, we don't see how anyone could be a slave trader with a clear conscience. Relatively speaking, we don't think we are very great sinners. Therefore, we don't feel a great need for God's grace. I read the comment of a polling expert once who said that the average person thinks he is better than the average person.

Even if we haven't sinned drastically in a public way, we have still sinned drastically. And sometimes it takes just as long for us to see the depth of our personal sin as it did for John Newton to see the depth of his public sin. In either case, grace is needed to break through and allow us to say, "but now I see."

The reason I try never to stray from the Bible in my preaching and teaching is that it is a mirror to reveal who we really are (James 1:23). We see either our self-righteousness or our sin, and respond accordingly (Luke 18:9–14). Our religious self-righteousness can blind us to who we truly are. When we read Scripture, we can see the examples of self-righteousness and see ourselves in them— and cry out for the grace of God.

The apostle Paul came to understand spiritual blindness as well as anyone ever has. He was complicit in the murder of Christians before he became one himself after being confronted by Christ (Acts 9). He thought he was doing the will and work of God by persecuting Christians, but he later realized it was because he was blind and could not see. It was not that he "did not see," but that he "could not see."

In Romans 2, Paul takes up the subject of religion, reminding his readers that even religious people can be blind to spiritual truth. In chapter one of Romans, Paul said that God has poured out His wrath upon a sinful human race. And lest anyone think that a veneer of religion is sufficient to cover human sin, he writes the message of chapter two. We need to start seeing ourselves as God sees us, not as we want to be seen by Him and others.

Paul gives six principles that show how God judges when He looks at the heart of man. We can make these principles a grid by which we judge our own hearts.

GOD'S JUDGMENT IS ACCORDING TO REALITY (VERSE 1)

God sees us as we really are: "And there is no creature hidden from His sight, but all things are naked and open to the eyes of Him to whom we must give account" (Hebrews 4:13). Paul says in Romans 2:1 that we are guilty of the same things of which we judge others to be guilty. Hypocritical religious leaders would condemn their followers for their sin while failing to judge themselves guilty as well.

Perhaps all preachers and leaders have been guilty of the sin of double standards at one time or another. We know we cannot be perfect, but we can be honest and transparent and empathetic. Hypocrites lose all credibility when they judge others without judging themselves.

A fable is told of an Indonesian farmer traveling on a path through the jungle when he saw a tiger's tail visible in the undergrowth ahead of him. Knowing the tiger was waiting to pounce on him, the farmer put down his scythe, ran forward and grabbed the tiger's tail. The tiger tried to get loose, but the farmer held on. A holy man appeared on the trail and the farmer pleaded with him to take the scythe and kill the tiger. The holy man refused, citing the tenets of his religion not to kill any living thing. The farmer convinced the holy man to hold the tiger by the tail while he killed him. The holy man agreed. Once free, the farmer picked up his scythe and turned to walk away. When the holy man cried out for him to kill the tiger—not to leave him in the predicament—the farmer replied that he was sorry, he couldn't. He had been converted to the holy man's view not to kill any living thing. The holy man, of course, was guilty of hypocrisy. He refused to kill when it was another's life at stake, but sanctioned the killing when it was his life in danger.[1]

What we believe is often revealed as being inconsistent and hypocritical.

God's Judgment Is According to Integrity (Verses 2–3)

A case could be made that John Newton shouldn't have been held accountable for his sin of slave-trading since it was a cultural norm in his day. I have considered that argument but have to believe that, deep in his soul, Newton knew it was wrong. He allowed the culture's blindness to give him permission to continue doing what he knew was wrong.

God didn't hold Newton accountable for what the culture said was acceptable, but for what is the truth. And He views us the same way.

God's Judgment Is According to Opportunity (Verses 4–5)

God is saying to religious leaders, "Don't think that your special privilege of being knowledgeable in religion is going to cause Me to see you in any way other than as you are." If you have a hard heart toward God, "you are treasuring up for yourself wrath in the day of wrath and revelation of the righteous judgment of God" (verse 5).

Many Christians in America were raised with every spiritual advantage and privilege. The average home in America has 5.2 Bibles. We have all the latest versions and translations. We'll never be able to stand before God and claim ignorance of His Word. But there are many in our world who have not had the Bible available to them. And we who have had the privileged background are going to be held to a higher standard than the spiritually underprivileged—not in terms of our salvation, but in terms of our faithfulness.

If you have the opportunity to learn about God and what He expects and you don't take it, you'll be held accountable for that one day.

God's Judgment Is According to Morality (Verses 6–10)

The moral judgment of God is confirmed in the Old Testament by Jeremiah 17:10: "I, the Lord, search the heart, I test the mind, even to give every man according to his ways, according to the fruit of his doings."

It's possible that those who have so many spiritual privileges—like Christians who attend sound churches in America—can miss the real issue. The blessings of God are nice, but they are not the heart of the faith. Paul was saying to religious leaders of his day (primarily Jewish leaders with whom he contended over the faith) that just because they had the Law of Moses, that did not make them righteous before God. It's wonderful to have and know the Word of God, but what's really important is doing it! Too often, especially in our day, there is a huge gap between what we know and what we do.

A well-known pastor friend of mine confessed to me that he thought the large glass doors at the front of his church were actually not doors but giant erasers—as people walked out through the doors after a Sunday service, they erased everything they had just heard and learned. He often got discouraged over the disconnect between what Christians in his church, and churches in general, were being taught and how they were living. Our greatest enemy is over-familiarity with the truth—becoming comfortable with it like an old friend around whom we can "be ourselves." Instead, we ought to be studying the Word in order to do it. It doesn't matter if we are in the Word if the Word is not in us, transforming our lives.

GOD'S JUDGMENT IS ACCORDING TO IMPARTIALITY (VERSES 11–15)

Verse 11 is a complete summary of this entire section: "For there is no partiality with God." What this means is that everyone stands on equal footing before God in terms of His judgment and in terms of His grace. God is not at all partial to anyone; He doesn't play favorites.

If you're a parent, you know that your children have studied you. Mine certainly studied my wife and me. They knew what they could ask for and when—and what they couldn't. They knew when to come and tell me things I might not want to hear—mainly, when I was in the best of moods. And now I'm seeing my grandchildren do the same thing with my (now-adult) children. All children do it!

But the truth is, we cannot work God! We cannot get an edge on Him in hopes He will act favorably toward us. God doesn't have a good side and a bad side. God has only one side: His holy side. He's never partial and doesn't have moods that change like we do. Peter made this very clear: "And if you call on the Father, who without partiality judges according to each one's work . . ." (1 Peter

1:17; see also Deuteronomy 10:17; Acts 10:34; Ephesians 6:9; Colossians 3:25).

Paul reminds religious leaders, those who like to feel elevated because of their religious credentials, that they are not better than others. They may try to give the impression that they have the inside track to God because of their position, but they do not. God shows no partiality; He judges everyone exactly the same. No one has a better standing before God than anyone else.

GOD'S JUDGMENT IS ACCORDING TO CERTAINTY (VERSE 16)

In this last verse Paul says, "in the day when God will judge the secrets of men by Jesus Christ . . . ." There are some secrets in the hearts of men that they believe will be carried with them to their graves. Fears, dreams, shameful things, questions—all of us have things that we've never told anybody. But God knows them all. To Him our hearts are an open book. If we are ever tempted to engage in posturing before God—trying to present ourselves differently from who we are—we should forget it. God knows our heart; we are not fooling Him.

Are you familiar with Hans Christian Anderson's story, "The Emperor's New Clothes?" The emperor was very concerned about his outward appearance, about what people thought of him. Some con men offered to weave him a beautiful and costly garment that would be visible only to those who were wise and pure in heart. The emperor accepted their offer and the con men sat before their looms pretending to be weaving the new garment. The king, growing impatient, sent his officials to check on the "weavers'" progress. The officials did not want to appear unwise and impure in heart, so they reported that the garment was progressing nicely. Then the king went, and saw nothing; but he wanted to appear wise and pure in heart, so he gave the weavers medals for their fine work.

Finally, on the day of a grand parade, the weavers pretended to dress the king in his garment, took their money, and fled the town. All the town applauded the naked king, not wanting to appear unwise and impure, until a child, in his innocence, cried out, "The emperor has no clothes!" An innocent remark by a child who didn't know there was a charade going on stripped away the pretense of all the adults and exposed the fraud.

That is the pretense and blindness Paul is describing in Romans, chapter two. We pretend to be dressed in our self-righteous religiosity. We believe our own beliefs can make reality something it is not. We believe that the lie we are living is the truth. And then Paul, like the child in the crowd, strips away the charade and exposes our nakedness before God.

In the Word of God, we see ourselves for who we are—the way God sees us. Once we are exposed, we lean solely on the grace of God to cover who we are with the righteous robes of Christ.

Note:

1. Summarized from John Phillips, *Exploring Romans* (Chicago: Moody Press, 1969), 37–38.

1. Compare Romans 2:1–3 with Matthew 7:1–5.

   a. What is Jesus' command in Matthew 7:1?

   b. In light of verse 2, how does verse 1 become more of a warning than a command?

   c. Create a hypothetical (or actual) example of a "speck" versus a "plank." What small thing might someone criticize another for when that same issue is large in his own life?

   d. Why is it hypocritical to discuss the speck in someone else's life without dealing with the plank in our life?

   e. What is the proper order of events given by Jesus in verse 5?

   f. How do Jesus' words in verse 2 echo the Old Testament principle found in Exodus 21:23–25?

2. Read Romans 2:12–16.

   a. Identify the two groups of people in the world Paul mentions in verse 12:

      • Those with the (Mosaic) Law: _____

      • Those without the (Mosaic) Law: _____

b. Are both groups going to be judged? (verse 12)

c. What is more important—to have (hear) the Law or to do the Law? (verse 13)

d. What standard do those without God's written revelation use for their lives? (verse 14)

e. How will God use their own standards to pass judgment on them? (verses 15–16)

f. What does that say about differing standards of judgment for different people? How will standards differ for a person in America who owns a Bible and a person in a primitive jungle setting who does not?

g. Why is it unwise to ignore the revelation God has given to you?

h. What role can your conscience play in keeping you from judging others unrighteously? (verse 15)

3. Read Romans 14:1–23.

a. Over what kind of matters were the Christians in Rome judging one another? (verses 1–3, 5)

b. What is the heart of Paul's argument? (verse 4)

c. What should Christians do in making decisions about debatable matters? (verse 5b)

d. For whom should all our actions be done? (verse 6)

e. Why is it foolish to judge another for his beliefs and choices? (verses 10, 12)

f. Instead of judging, what should we resolve to do? (verse 13)

g. What was Paul's opinion about the matter of some foods being "unclean"? (verse 14)

h. What freedom would he give to a Christian who disagreed? (verse 14)

i. What additional step would he take so as not to cause that Christian to sin? (verse 15)

j. What is more important: Our beliefs on non-essential matters, or our brother? (verse 15b)

k. What is the essence of the kingdom of God? (verse 17)

l. How do judging and disputes destroy the essence of the kingdom?

m. What should our goal be in the church? (verse 19)

n. What practical advice does Paul give in verse 21?

o. Why should one live with faith instead of doubts about lifestyle choices? (verses 22–23)

DID YOU KNOW?

Paul had never been to Rome when he wrote his letter to that church. Therefore, his admonitions about hypocrisy and judgmental practices of leaders were not addressed specifically to the leaders in Rome. It is thought that Paul laid out this most exhaustive theological overview for the Rome church because of its potential place in his strategic plans. The church at Antioch had been the initial sending church for his missionary trips; but now that he wanted to go to Spain and beyond (Romans 15:24, 28; 2 Corinthians 10:16), Paul likely saw Rome as being his next base of operations. Unfortunately, he was ultimately martyred in Rome. There is no direct evidence of his ever having reached Spain.

THE COMFORTING PROVISION OF GRACE

Romans 5:1–11

*In this lesson we learn what becomes ours
when we receive the grace of God.*

OUTLINE

We know that the grace of God is what makes our salvation possible. But many Christians do not realize it is the grace of God that makes our Christian life possible as well. Everything we need to begin and continue our walk with Jesus—peace, encouragement, and more—is by grace.

   I. **We Have a New Peace for Our Contentment**

   II. **We Have a New Principle for Our Encouragement**

   III. **We Have a New Promise for Our Enjoyment**

   IV. **We Have a New Process for Our Development**
   - A. From Tribulation to Perseverance
   - B. From Perseverance to Character
   - C. From Character to Hope

   V. **We Have a New Power for Our Enrichment**

   VI. **We Have a New Plan for Our Advancement**

   VII. **We Have a New Purpose for Our Excitement**

One of the greatest illustrations of grace I have ever seen was at a Moody Bible Institute Pastors' Conference where the late Dr. E. V. Hill was the speaker. He was speaking on "What Do You Have if You Have Jesus?" One of his points was that Jesus does things for us out of the goodness of His heart—things we don't expect and certainly don't deserve.

Off to the side of the stage was a table with a stack of books that were to be given as gifts later in the meeting. During his message, Dr. Hill would wander over to that table, pick up one of the books, and just sail it out into the audience of pastors where it would be caught be some lucky attendee. He did that nearly ten times during his message just to illustrate that grace comes from God freely, often, and sometimes when we least expect it.

In Romans 5:1–11 Paul gives us a list of things that come to us by God's grace—gifts that flow from the goodness of His heart to us.

WE HAVE A NEW PEACE FOR OUR CONTENTMENT (VERSE 1)

The first thing that becomes ours with grace is peace with God. The Bible says we are enemies of God before we become a Christian (Romans 5:10). After becoming a Christian, the hostilities cease. Even if the hostility was passive or benign on our part—if we were a respectable person trying to live a moral life—it was still hostility based on our sinful desire to be the ruler of our own life.

I often hear new believers say they feel like "a load" was lifted off their shoulders when they accepted Christ. That's the load of hostility that vanishes when we make Christ the Lord of our life. Instead of clinched fists raised against God, we now extend open hands to Him in a gesture of fellowship and reconciliation (Colossians 1:21–22a). Paul says in Philippians 4:6–7 that the peace of God "surpasses all understanding."

Sometimes non-Christians don't understand how Christians can have such peace in the midst of life's up's and down's. It's hard to understand the peace *of* God without having experienced peace *with* God.

Paul often introduced and closed his letters with the phrase, "Grace to you and peace from God our Father and the Lord Jesus Christ" (for example, Romans 1:7; 1 Corinthians 1:3; 2 Corinthians 1:2;

Galatians 1:3). Notice the order: Grace, then peace. First comes the grace of God and the peace of God follows. How grateful we should be for the grace of God that results in our experiencing the peace of God in a world of unrest!

WE HAVE A NEW PRINCIPLE FOR OUR ENCOURAGEMENT (VERSE 2a)

When we become Christians, it's as if a gate is opened allowing us to have "access by faith into this grace in which we stand" (verse 2a). The grace that saves us is the same grace that allows us to stand by faith in our Christian life. "Standing" in the grace of God means that grace is our foundation, our environment, our life-support system. This idea is similar to what Paul says in Acts 17:28: "in [Christ] we live and move and have our being . . . ." Grace is not just the source of our salvation, it is the source of our entire life.

WE HAVE A NEW PROMISE FOR OUR ENJOYMENT (VERSE 2b)

Not only do we gain peace and encouragement from grace, we also get new joy: We "rejoice in hope of the glory of God."

In just two verses, Paul has given us the past, present, and future of the grace of God. We get peace relative to our past sins; we get access to grace for our present life; and we get the hope of glory for our future. Our lives have grace as bookends on both ends.

The word "rejoice" in the Greek language literally means "to boast." Normally, boasting has a negative connotation—it sounds arrogant or prideful. But in the New Testament, it is used in the sense of boasting in Christ (2 Corinthians 12:9). The prophet Jeremiah says it as well as anyone:

Thus says the Lord:

"Let not the wise man glory in his wisdom,
Let not the mighty man glory in his might,
Nor let the rich man glory in his riches;
But let him who glories glory in this,
That he understands and knows Me,
That I am the Lord, exercising lovingkindness,
    judgment, and righteousness in the earth.
For in these I delight," says the Lord. (9:23–24)

Jeremiah says, "If you want to boast, boast in God." Paul affirms this idea in 1 Corinthians 1:31: "'He who glories, let him glory in the Lord.'" When was the last time you boasted to someone about how great the Lord is and what He has done in your life?

WE HAVE A NEW PROCESS FOR OUR DEVELOPMENT (VERSES 3–4)

So far everything has been rosy about the benefits of grace in our lives. Now Paul takes a turn in a different direction in talking about how God works for our spiritual development: "And not only that, but we also glory in tribulations, knowing that tribulation produces perseverance; and perseverance, character; and character, hope." When is the last time you gloried in your tribulations? It is the gift of God by grace to allow us to go through times of suffering and trouble. It's not punishment—it's a gift of grace that He uses to cause us to mature.

I met a Christian man recently who shared with me a bit about his family. His daughter had been deaf since birth and he, at age forty, had been diagnosed with an incurable neurological disease. But I observed, in spite of his difficulties, that he was a man who was strong at the center of his life, who had a strong relationship with the Lord, who loved his family, and had an evident maturity. I believe he got that way by responding to the grace of God in his life, allowing troubles to develop him instead of destroy him.

There are three steps in the process of development via troubles.

From Tribulation to Perseverance

First, tribulation gives us the ability to persevere: "tribulation produces perseverance." Perseverance means to live under the pressure God has allowed and not continually be looking for a way out. It means not to ask, "Why did You allow this?" but to ask, "What do You want me to learn from this?" Peter says that trials prove the genuineness of our faith that will result in praise to God "at the revelation of Jesus Christ" (1 Peter 1:6–7).

Sometimes God does more than just allow trouble—He sends it to reveal our self-sufficiency and to increase our dependence on Him. How else are we to learn that we don't have all the answers we thought we had? It is God's grace that reveals what we lack and creates situations whereby we can learn what we don't know.

From Perseverance to Character

Second, Paul says perseverance produces character. Character means we develop the characteristics of Christ, characteristics of godliness, the ability to respond to life with a godly perspective and godly wisdom. Pressure in Christ's life moved Him to say, "nevertheless not My will, but Yours, be done" (Luke 22:42). And it will do the same for us if we respond to God's grace.

From Character to Hope

Finally, Paul says that character produces hope. In 2 Corinthians 4:17, he says that "our light affliction, which is but for a moment, is working for us a far more exceeding and eternal weight of glory." Our affliction is light compared to the "weight of glory" that is to be ours, and it is "but for a moment" compared to the eternity of glory in heaven. Our troubles on this earth are child's play in light of the great glory to be experienced forever in eternity (Romans 8:18).

Like you, I have had my share of problems in this life. And looking back, I can see how they were all used by the Lord to teach me perseverance, character, and hope. I would not want to go through them again, but I thank God they were part of His plan for my life. The key is to yield to the pressure and let it shape you into that which God is making you to be.

WE HAVE A NEW POWER FOR OUR ENRICHMENT (VERSES 5–8)

"Hope does not disappoint," Paul says, "because the love of God has been poured out in our hearts by the Holy Spirit who was given to us" (verse 5).

When we become Christians, part of the grace of God toward us is the gift of the Holy Spirit. When we receive Christ, we receive the Holy Spirit as well. The Holy Spirit acts like an automatic "sin alarm" system. The things we used to do before we were saved that didn't bother us at all . . . now an alarm goes off in us when we even consider doing them. That is the Holy Spirit tweaking us to remind us that we are about to sin against the holiness of God.

When Paul says the Spirit has "poured" the love of God into our hearts, he uses a term that suggests such an abundance that there is not sufficient room to contain it. We don't just have a little of the love of God by the Spirit, we have love that is overflowing! This, I believe, is the overflow that every new Christian experiences when they first come to know Christ and know the Spirit's presence. His power makes a marked difference in our life.

This dimension of love through the Holy Spirit (note that love is the first in Paul's list of the fruit of the Spirit in Galatians 5:22–23) is so important because there are some people in your life that only the Holy Spirit can love. Perhaps your flesh still responds negatively to some people you encounter, but God's Spirit can give you love for them that you lack naturally. That supernatural love is what Christ desired for His followers (John 17).

WE HAVE A NEW PLAN FOR OUR ADVANCEMENT (VERSES 9–10)

Many Christians live under the mistaken notion that having been saved by grace, it is now up to them to maintain their salvation; that grace was to forgive them and save them, not to keep them for the rest of their lives. But Paul says differently: "Much more then, having now been justified by His blood, we shall be saved from wrath through Him" (verse 9).

The truth is, we cannot any more maintain our own salvation than we could attain our own salvation. We cannot live by the energy of the flesh any more than we could have been saved by good works. We live the Christian life the same way we entered it: by grace. In verse 10, Paul reasons that if God extended grace to us when we were His enemies, how much more will He extend grace to us so we might continue to mature as we walk with Christ. It has been stated by many that the Christian life is not difficult—it's impossible! We need the grace of God to live out the salvation into which we have entered.

If you struggle with maintaining victory in your Christian life, perhaps it is because you are trying to live it in your own strength. If you will daily ask God for grace to live, just as you asked Him for grace to be saved, you will receive it. He will pour out His power into you through the Holy Spirit. His grace will be sufficient for you on a moment-by-moment basis as you walk by faith, not by sight (2 Corinthians 5:7). This is the new plan for your advancement that comes with the grace of God and the presence of the Spirit.

WE HAVE A NEW PURPOSE FOR OUR EXCITEMENT (VERSE 11)

Finally, Paul says "we also rejoice in God through our Lord Jesus Christ, through whom we have now received the reconciliation."

I think there are some Christians who didn't get the memo about our freedom to rejoice in Christ. If asked, they say they have the joy of the Lord, but their countenance doesn't seem to show it. I've actually had non-Christians say to me, "If Christianity is like some Christians I know, please protect me! I don't want to catch that disease!" Isn't that a shame? The joy that is available to us in Christ should be attracting people to the Savior. Sadly, some Christians think it is their calling to be the quality control experts in Christianity, always pointing out what is wrong instead of rejoicing in what is right.

Don't misunderstand—I'm not suggesting doctrinal compromise for the sake of getting along. On the basics of the faith, we remain unmoved. But there is lots of room in Christianity to express our faith in diverse ways and not let our joy be robbed because we disagree with some people. Disagreements and criticism over non-essential matters is not evidence of the Spirit of Christ.

I have a friend who is a new Christian and brings some baggage from his past into his new walk with Christ. Because he is a well-known businessman in the community, I have taken some heat from some Christians for putting my arm around this brother and supporting him in his new relationship with God. While it's sad that I've been criticized, he told me that his son, who is not a Christian, had seen how he was being treated by some in the Christian community. "Dad," his son told him, "I don't know any of your former non-Christian friends who would have treated you like the Christians are treating you. If that's what Christianity is about, you can forget about me becoming one."

If you are a true Christian, one who understands the grace of God that saved you, you will have joy in your life, rejoicing over all that God is doing in saints and sinners alike. You won't criticize and pick at your brothers and sisters in Christ. You'll rejoice and celebrate, both in church and in the community. If you are more comfortable hearing a funeral dirge in church than a song of celebration, you need to check your "joy meter" and see what it is registering. We need to continually be in a state of mind that says, "Lord Jesus, thank You for loving me, for making me a recipient of Your grace. Thank You for giving me the grace to live every day with joy in what can be a difficult life. Your grace always abounds and is always enough! For that, I praise Your name!"

Fifty-five years after becoming a Christian, John Newton was still amazed by the grace of God. He composed a prayer in a letter to his wife, part of which said, "Well may I say with wonder and gratitude, 'Why me, O Lord, why me?'"[1]

He never got over the fact that God's grace had apprehended him while in a life of sin and debauchery—and neither should we. If you have not marveled lately at the grace of God that saves you and keeps you, might not now be a good time? And if you have not yet experienced the grace of God, would this also not be the day to do so? When you get grace, you get more than you can imagine.

Note:

1. Richard Cecil, *Memoirs of the Rev. John Newton*, Ed. Marylynn Rouse, (Ross-shire, Great Britain: Christian Focus Publications, 2000), 59.

1. What is God's throne called in Hebrews 4:16?

   a. What correlation do you find between the admonishment to approach the throne freely (boldly) and the fact that it is a throne of grace?

   b. What connection do you find between grace as the ongoing power in our Christian life and the throne of grace being connected with prayer?

   c. What else does the verse mention as being received at the throne of grace?

   d. Note the three blessings grouped together in the following verses:

      • 1 Timothy 1:2

      • 2 Timothy 1:2

      • Titus 1:4

      • 2 John 3

   e. What is the connection between grace and mercy in continuing to live the Christian life?

f. In prayer, we ask for forgiveness for the past and strength for the future. How do mercy and grace cover both of these parts of our spiritual life?

2. In Zechariah 12:10, what does God promise to pour out upon the Jews one day?

   a. Who is the "One they have pierced"?

   b. And what will they do when they recognize who He is?

   c. How is this similar to what happens to us when the grace of God allows us to see who Jesus is for the first time?

   d. Why is the Holy Spirit referred to here, and in Hebrews 10:29, as the "Spirit of grace"?

3. How is Luke 2:40 an example of the role of grace in our ongoing spiritual maturity and development?

   a. What kind of words came from the mouth of Jesus? (Psalm 45:2; Luke 4:22)

b. What was Christ full of? What does it mean to be full

of _____. (John 1:14)

c. How did grace come through Jesus Christ? (John 1:17; Romans 5:15)

d. What connection was there between Christ's words and life and the Holy Spirit? (John 3:34)

e. What grace connection do you find between 1 Peter 1:10, 1 Corinthians 1:4, and Ephesians 2:7?

f. Why is it right to praise the "glorious grace" of God in light of what it has brought to us? (Ephesians 1:6)

4. What evidence of grace was there in the apostles' lives after their salvation? (Acts 4:33)

a. Based on this lesson's points, how would you describe the "riches" of the grace of God? (Ephesians 1:7; 2:7)

b. What was it that enabled the Corinthian Christians to give generously to the needy? (2 Corinthians 9:14)

c. What enables you to serve with your spiritual gift? (1 Peter 4:10)

d. What made it possible for Paul to endure despite his sufferings? (2 Corinthians 12:9)

e. What allows you to overcome sin in your life? (Romans 5:20)

5. What can you conclude about the necessity for grace after salvation?

DID YOU KNOW?

John Newton's tombstone reads, "John Newton, Clerk, once an infidel and libertine, a servant of slaves in Africa, was, by the rich mercy of our Lord and Saviour Jesus Christ, preserved, restored, pardoned, and appointed to preach the faith he had long labored to destroy." When African tribes warred against one another, the victorious tribe bartered its captives to slave traders in exchange for weapons, ammunition, blankets, metal, liquor, and other goods. Captives were packed into the bottom of slave ships, as many as 600 at a time, for the journey across the Atlantic. Mortality rates on the voyage ran as high as 20 percent, the sick and dead being thrown overboard.

THE CONNECTING POINT OF GRACE

Acts 9:1–9

*In this lesson we see an example of
the converting power of grace.*

OUTLINE

We hear a lot today about "seeker sensitive" churches and "seeker driven" services. But the Bible says that no one seeks after God. Yet there is a Seeker, and His name is Jesus. Jesus sought out Saul, and he was converted in an instant because of the powerful grace of God in his life.

   I. Saul the Hunter

  II. Saul the Hunted
   - A. Confrontation
   - B. Conviction
   - C. Conversion
   - D. Consecration
   - E. Communion

 III. Saul the Humbled
   - A. The Power of Grace in Our Salvation
   - B. The Pursuit of God in Our Salvation

W e've been focusing on a few key phrases from John Newton's famous hymn; and in this lesson, we'll think about his words, "How precious did that grace appear, the hour I first believed."

Do you remember the hour you first believed? Where you were, what the circumstances were, and how you felt? That's a once-in-a-lifetime experience that you will never relive except in your memories. It's a moment when, after being pursued by God's grace, you gave in and allowed the weight of sin and guilt to roll off your back.

John Newton could remember the hour he first believed because it was so dramatic. He was a man who went out of his way to find new ways to sin. He blasphemed God, lived a wanton life, and tried to get others to do the same. And yet the hour came when he believed in the very God he had cursed.

He was working on a slave ship named the *Greyhound*. On March 21, 1748, he was asleep in the hold of the ship when it began to be tossed by a violent storm. He spent nine hours manning the pumps, trying to get the water out of the ship so it wouldn't sink. He was then assigned to the helm of the ship until midnight. Alone at the helm, he struggled to keep the ship on course in the storm. But he was struggling with something else: his unbelief and what he had been taught about the Savior as a child. But he was convinced at that moment that he had sinned so terribly all his life that he couldn't possibly be a candidate for salvation.

By the next day, the storm was weakening; and Newton wondered if God was showing them favor. A copy of the New Testament made it through the storm, and he began reading it. As is true with most people, going through the storms of life makes you much more spiritually sensitive.

Newton read the book of Luke. When he got to the eleventh chapter, the thirteenth verse, he found Jesus saying these words: ". . . how much more will your heavenly Father give the Holy Spirit to those who ask Him!" He decided to take Jesus at his word. He prayed and read for several hours, asking for the Holy Spirit to be given to him.

When his ship arrived in Ireland four weeks later, he made a note in his journal that on the day of the terrible storm—March 21, 1748— he gave his heart to Christ and became a Christian. His words were

"I stood in need of an Almighty Savior and I found one in the New Testament."[1]

From that moment on, Newton was a changed man. Fifty-seven years later, on the same day as his salvation—March 21—he was eighty years old, almost blind, and could hardly move. He hadn't written anything in a long time, but struggled to make a final journal entry: "Not well able to write; but I endeavor to observe the return of this day with humiliation, and prayer, and praise."[2]

Half a century after his conversion, John Newton was still celebrating the amazing grace that had changed his life. He was like the apostle Paul in that sense, never getting over the fact that grace found and changed him. Newton's conversion and Paul's were very similar—sudden, dramatic, utterly life-changing, and never to be forgotten.

Paul's conversion, the subject of this lesson, is recorded in Acts 9. Paul tells the story of his conversion in Acts 22 to a mob of Jews, and again in Acts 26 to a group of Roman rulers. So there are three distinct accounts of Paul's dramatic conversion to Christ. Besides Christ Himself, we have more details about the life of the apostle Paul than any other figure in the New Testament.

Next to Jesus Christ, Paul is the most influential person who has ever lived. He wrote approximately half the New Testament. He was the architect of the early church, the original missionary, and a brilliant intellect whose writings and teachings shaped much of Western civilization. His letter to the church at Rome is the greatest theological treatise ever written.

It only stands to reason that Paul's testimony would be unique, given the uniqueness of his person.

SAUL THE HUNTER

Paul (his Jewish name was Saul) thought he was doing God a favor by persecuting the followers of Jesus. He was a zealous Pharisee who viewed Christianity as a blasphemy and a heresy. Paul was there at the stoning of Stephen, the first martyr of the infant church in Jerusalem (Acts 7:58). But he wasn't just a bystander, he was an active participant in the persecution of the church, making "havoc of the church, entering every house, and dragging off men and women, committing them to prison" (Acts 8:3). Then, in 9:1, we read that he went to the high priest to get authority to go to the synagogues in Damascus and take prisoner any Jewish believers in Jesus.

Paul had heard that some Jewish followers of Jesus had fled the persecution in Jerusalem and taken refuge in Damascus. He was not content to have them out of Jerusalem—he wanted them thrown into prison. He was granted letters of permission by the high priest and was on his way to Damascus to round up Jewish Christians when he met Christ. In Acts 22:4–5, Paul says he put both men and women in prison and went to Damascus with the intent of taking even more into custody and bringing them in chains to Jerusalem.

It is hard to believe that the Paul who gave his life for Christ is the same Saul intent on imprisoning the followers of Christ—but he was.

SAUL THE HUNTED

Sometimes we see people in this life, or at least hear about them, whom we think must surely be beyond the reach of God's grace. Had we known John Newton, we might have thought he was one. And had we known the apostle Paul (Saul of Tarsus) we might have thought he was another. After Paul became a Christian, the leaders of the church in Jerusalem were afraid of him because of his reputation as a persecutor (Acts 9:26).

But Paul went from being the hunter to the hunted as Jesus Christ set about to capture him with grace.

Confrontation

Combining Paul's three accounts in the Book of Acts, we learn all the details of what happened on the road to Damascus.

Christ's confrontation with Paul took place in the middle of the day when he saw "a light from heaven, brighter than the sun, shining around me and those who journeyed with me" (Acts 26:13). Saul's companions did not hear the voice that spoke to Paul out of the blazing light—the voice of Christ (Acts 22:9). The presence of Christ was very important to Paul because it is what qualified him later to become an apostle. One of the requirements was that every one of the original apostles had to have seen Jesus Christ, which Paul confirmed that he had in 1 Corinthians 9:1: "Have I not seen Jesus Christ our Lord?"

Conviction

Why does a person call another person's name twice? To get their attention, which is what Jesus did with Saul: "Saul, Saul, why are you persecuting Me" (Acts 9:4)? When I was a child and heard my mother say, "David Paul Jeremiah"—I knew I was in trouble and needed to get in the house in a hurry. Christ got Saul's attention in a hurry that day on the road to Damascus. When he heard his name being called, Saul knew two things for sure.

First, He knew that Jesus was alive, that the resurrection story was true. He immediately knew that his persecution of the Christians for claiming Jesus was alive had been wrong. Jesus was alive—He just called Paul's name . . . twice.

Second, he realized that when he persecuted the Christians, the pain he inflicted was being felt by Jesus Himself: "Saul, Saul, why are you persecuting *Me?*" (italics added) That should be a painful reminder to us that when we attack, criticize, or persecute other Christians with whom we have differences, we are attacking the Lord Himself.

Conversion

Though Saul had never met Jesus personally, Jesus confirms again that Saul has been persecuting Him: "I am Jesus, whom you are persecuting. It is hard for you to kick against the goads" (verse 5). That last phrase is not readily understandable in our day, but it refers to a prod used by herders in biblical times to keep cattle moving when being driven. But sometimes the cattle would kick against the pain of the prod—they would kick against the goad, the thing prodding them forward. So Jesus asked Saul, "Why are you kicking against the goad?"

What was goading Saul on? I believe there must have been something happening in his heart even before this encounter with Jesus. Remember, Saul stood by and watched Stephen, who had a face like an angel (Acts 6:15), be stoned to death. I can't help but believe that Saul was under conviction and he was fighting it—kicking against the goad. Jesus, in a sense, asks him why he is resisting the work that is going on in his heart.

So Saul's conversion was a direct encounter with Jesus Christ, though some have suggested other theories about what happened to him that day. Given the amazing change that took place in his life—from persecutor to apostle—it seems hard to deny the reality of what happened to him. Some people suggest he fell to the ground and hit his head, resulting in a vision of some sort. Others have suggested the bright sunlight reflected off the white buildings in Damascus blinded him. Others have suggested he had an epileptic fit, to which Charles Spurgeon replied, "O blessed epilepsy, would that every man . . . could have . . . that!"

None of these desperate attempts to explain away the reality of what happened can account for the ultimate change in Paul's life. He became, as he wrote in 2 Corinthians 5:17, "a new creation." He was totally transformed by the reality and power of God's grace.

A British barrister, or attorney at law, named Lord Lyttleton spent two years studying the account of Paul's conversion, thinking if he could disprove it, the whole New Testament would lack credibility. After two years, he became a Christian. The evidence was too strong that the biblical account of Paul's conversion was totally trustworthy.

Consecration

After identifying who was speaking to Him, Saul's first question following his conversion was one of consecration: "What do You want me to do?" Once he realized he was talking face to face with the Lord, he submitted himself to Christ's will. He became an obedient servant of the One he had been persecuting.

Communion

Saul spent the next three days in darkness and isolation. He was blind and was given nothing to eat or drink during that time. It's not clear what the purpose of that discipline was, but I believe it must have been a time of communion between Saul and Jesus— a time for Saul to think about what he had experienced without any other distractions. Sometimes solitude and fasting cause us to focus intently on spiritual issues like we otherwise could not do. Saul lay in the dark, thinking about the drastic change that had taken place in his life.

SAUL THE HUMBLED

There are two things that we learn about grace and God from Paul's experience and life.

The Power of Grace in Our Salvation

What would you or I do if we encountered someone who had been persecuting us the way Saul had been persecuting Jesus? We would likely react harshly. But when Jesus encountered Saul on the Damascus road, it was a moment of grace and forgiveness that Paul never forgot. Just as your own moment of grace, the saving moment in which you encountered Jesus, is etched indelibly in your memory, so was Paul's. All of us deserve to be judged when meeting Jesus, but instead we found grace and forgiveness.

Paul later wrote that he considered himself unworthy to be called an apostle because he persecuted the church of God. "By the grace of God I am what I am," he said (1 Corinthians 15:9–10). Paul understood he was not only not worthy to be saved, but certainly not worthy to become a key figure in the movement of the One he persecuted so vigorously. Yet God's grace was greater than all Saul's sin.

When writing to his protégé, Timothy, Paul called himself a former blasphemer, persecutor, and insolent man, "and the grace of our Lord was exceedingly abundant." He reiterates that Christ came into the world to save sinners, "of whom I am chief" (1 Timothy 1:12–15). It's no wonder Paul is called the "apostle of grace." He had experienced first hand the depths of sin and the heights of grace. He understood that he was the very kind of person Christ came into the world to seek and to save: the lost (Luke 19:10).

The Pursuit of God in Our Salvation

C. S. Lewis captured Paul's experience beautifully in describing his own salvation: "I never had the experience of looking for God. It was the other way around. He was the hunter and I was the deer. He stalked me, took unerring aim and fired."[3]

As I travel around the country preaching, I'm almost always asked (because people know I am from California), "What kind of church do you have? Is it 'seeker friendly?'" While that's a popular term today in church circles, I sometimes will reply by asking who the "seekers" are since Romans 3:11 says, "There is none who seeks after God." The true seeker is Jesus, not us. If I am "seeker friendly," it's because I am a friend of the only true Seeker, Jesus of Nazareth.

But it gets better—I'm also "seeker sensitive." Again, the seeker is Jesus, and I am trying to be sensitive to everything He says, everything He wants me to do. So, yes, I am Seeker sensitive because I live my life for the Seeker—whatever He wants me to do, I want to do.

I am Seeker friendly, Seeker sensitive, and am also Seeker driven. My whole life is motivated and energized by the Lord Jesus Christ. He is the driving force in my life. He is the reason I get up in the morning and feel an urgency to minister in His name during the day.

I was headed the opposite way in life until He sought me out and drew me to Himself. Not to live for Him for the rest of my life would be an unreasonable response to what He has done for me.

So it is not just the power of grace in our life that saves us—it is the pursuit of God as well. God pursues us, and His grace opens our eyes that we might see Him who has sought us out for Himself.

Is the Seeker seeking you? If you have been feeling conviction in your heart about your spiritual life, that's Him! The best thing you can do is to do what Saul did: Ask Him, "Lord, what do You want me to do?" I believe His answer will be, "Believe on the Lord Jesus Christ" (Acts 16:31).

Notes:

1. John Newton, *The Life and Spirituality of John Newton* (Vancouver: Regent College Publishing, 1998), 63.

2. Josiah Bull, *'But Now I See': The Life of John Newton* (Carlisle: Banner of Truth, 1998), 355.

3. C. S. Lewis, *Surprised by Joy* (San Diego: Harcourt Brace, 1956), 228.

1. Read Philippians 3:4–16.

   a. What is the subject of these verses? (verses 4, 7)

   b. What is Paul trying to show by listing all his Hebrew "credentials?" (verses 5–6)

   c. How far back did the rite of circumcision go? (verse 3; Genesis 17:12)

   d. Whose descendant was Paul since he had been circumcised? (Genesis 17:12)

   e. Whose descendant was Paul if he was of the stock of Israel? (verse 4; Genesis 32:28)

   f. Why did Benjamin, and later his tribe, have a special place in Israel? (Genesis 44:18–34)

   g. What famous king of Israel was also a Benjamite? (1 Samuel 9:1 ff.)

   h. What does the phrase "a Hebrew of the Hebrews" connote? (see Song of Songs 1:1; Daniel 2:37; 1 Timothy 6:15; Revelation 19:16).

i. To what religious party did Paul belong? (verse 5)

j. As a Pharisee in training, who was Paul's teacher? (Acts 22:3)

k. How did Paul demonstrate his zeal for God? (verse 6a)

l. How faithful was he following the Law of Moses? (verse 6b)

m. How did Paul count all these human accolades in comparison to knowing Christ? (verse 12)

n. What earthly term did he use to describe his pre-Christian accomplishments? (verse 8)

o. What kind of righteousness did Paul exchange for the self-righteousness he found through keeping the Law? (verse 9)

p. Instead of pressing toward Damascus to persecute Christians, what was Paul pressing toward? (verse 14)

q. What things similar to Paul's cultural heritage might one in America boast of?

r. What kind of "proud" religious background did you have before coming to Christ?

s. What advice does Paul have to those who might still be trusting in their fleshly achievements? (verse 15)

2. Read Acts 22:1–16.

a. Why did God seek out and choose Saul? (verse 14)

b. What was the ultimate purpose for Saul? (verses 15, 21)

c. What was the first thing Saul did as a new believer? (verse 16)

d. How did he describe his previous vengeance against the followers of Jesus? (verses 4, 19)

e. To whom was Paul giving his testimony? (see Acts 21:30–40)

f. How did they receive his testimony when he was finished? (Acts 22:22–25)

3. Read Acts 26:1–23.

a. Before whom is Paul testifying this time? (verses 2, 24–25)

b. What do you learn in this testimony about Paul's participation in the death of Christians? (verse 10)

c. What did he force Christians to do? (verse 11)

d. How did Paul describe his feelings toward the Christians? (verse 11b)

e. To whom was Paul sent—Jews or Gentiles? (verse 17)

f. For what purpose? (verse 18)

g. If you are a Gentile, are you a recipient of the message Jesus commissioned Saul to proclaim?

DID YOU KNOW?

In Acts 9:2, Luke refers to Christians as those "who were of the Way." "The Way" was a first-century label for the movement comprised of the followers of Jesus (Acts 19:9, 23; 24:14, 22). Luke also tells us that followers of Jesus were first referred to as Christians in Antioch, but we don't know exactly when (Acts 11:26). The formal term "The Way" may have arisen from Jesus' statement in which He called Himself "the way, the truth, and the life" (John 14:6). Or it may refer to the phrase "the way of salvation" or "the way of God" or "the way of the Lord" (Acts 16:17; 18:25–26).

THE CONFUSING PARADOX OF GRACE

2 Corinthians 4:7–11, 17–18; 12:7–10

*In this lesson we discover that when we are weak,
grace can make us strong.*

OUTLINE

The kingdom of God is filled with numerous paradoxes: To live we must die, to receive we must give, and to be strong we must be weak. It is only when we find ourselves without strength that the grace of God allows the power of Jesus Christ to be strong through us.

I. The Requirement of Grace for the Christian Life

II. The Resource of Grace for the Christian Life

III. The Result of Grace in the Christian Life
   A. The Grace of God Produces Power
   B. The Grace of God Provides Perspective
   C. The Grace of God Promotes Perseverance
   D. The Grace of God Promotes Praise

In this lesson we turn to another famous line of John Newton's "Amazing Grace": "Through many dangers, toils, and snares, I have already come." You and I can identify with that line. In fact, there is nobody who hasn't experienced "dangers, toils, and snares" to one degree or another in this life. John Newton, however, experienced more than most.

Once on a hunting outing he was scrambling up the hill with his rifle slung over his shoulder when it went off, blowing a hole in his hat, almost killing him. Another time, in Liberia, Newton was about to row up a river when his captain replaced him with another sailor. Later they got word that the boat had sunk and the sailor had drowned. Another time he hosted a party at which he became intoxicated and he almost drowned. John Newton escaped death on more than one occasion, giving him credibility in saying that he had come through many dangers, indeed.

But even John Newton's brushes with death and lifestyle of narrow escapes, could not rival those of the apostle Paul. He was constantly being chased, harassed, beaten, imprisoned, and ridiculed. In 2 Corinthians 11, Paul chronicled these events in a long list that is hard to believe. Once when I was in the hospital, I got a "Get Well" card from a friend that had the list from 2 Corinthians 11 on the front of the card. Then inside it said this: "So, how've you been?"

That was the most refreshing card I received during my whole illness because it made me realize that what I was going through was nothing compared to what the apostle Paul went through in his life. I was undergoing difficulties for a few days, whereas he did it daily for decades! Paul's two lengthy passages about his "dangers, toils, and snares" in 2 Corinthians should be on the must-read list of every Christian (2 Corinthians 6:3–10; 11:16–29).

Someone once told me, "In this life you're either headed for trouble, in trouble, or heading out of trouble." Trouble is part of life, and the Christian who does not realize this is setting himself up for terrible disappointment. To experience trouble in this life is to prove your humanity (Job 5:7).

THE REQUIREMENT OF GRACE FOR THE CHRISTIAN LIFE (VERSES 4:7–9)

Why do we need grace to face dangers, toils, and snares? Because we carry the life of Jesus around in earthen (delicate) human vessels. We are "hard pressed . . . perplexed . . . struck down," but not "crushed . . . in despair . . . [or] destroyed." And it is by grace that we are not.

Almighty God sent His Son, Jesus Christ, into the world in a frail human body just like yours and mine. God in a human body! It's an amazing thought. And the same is true of us. God is in us (we are not God, but He lives in us through the Spirit), in our earthen vessels—literally, "clay pots." In Paul's day, clay pots were the common vessels used by everyone. Their value was determined by their contents—empty, they had little value since they were so common.

We are common clay pots made valuable by the presence of God in us. And we are subject to difficult times in this world. Most people experience more problems after becoming a Christian than they did before because they are now going against the world and against their old nature. A lot of people were surprised several years ago when I fought cancer, thinking pastors weren't supposed to get sick. The reason I got sick is that I'm human. Sickness is a human condition. Sometimes clay pots crack and sometimes they break, and only the grace of God can help you deal with it when it happens.

In 2 Corinthians 12, Paul tells about a particular kind of trouble he experienced: a thorn in his flesh, "a messenger of Satan," to keep him humble (verses 7–10). Why did he need to be reminded about humility? Because he was allowed to visit the third heaven and receive revelations that no one else had received. He saw heaven through his human eyes (2 Corinthians 12:1–6). To make him ever mindful of the need not to feel exalted about that experience, God allowed Paul to be afflicted in some way by Satan.

THE RESOURCE OF GRACE FOR THE CHRISTIAN LIFE (VERSES 12:8–9a)

Three times Paul asked God to remove Satan's buffeting from him. God answered Paul's prayer—just not in the way he expected. Paul needed grace to endure the affliction he was experiencing, and grace is what he received from the Lord. The Lord Jesus said to him, "My grace is sufficient for you, for My strength is made perfect in weakness." Instead of taking away Paul's thorn in the flesh, he was given grace to live with it. Paul found that God's grace was "sufficient." The verb "to be sufficient" is in the present tense in verse nine, meaning it is a present, ongoing reality. God's grace is always sufficient to meet our need.

We have not begun to tap into the reality of just how abundant God's grace is. If every Christian in the world needed the maximum amount of grace at the same time, there would be no shortage. If every sinner in the world repented and came to Christ at the same time, there would be no shortage. God's grace is as infinite as God Himself. God has sufficient grace for every need you will ever have. Grace is the resource God provides for living the Christian life in a world of trouble.

I remember saying, at the end of a difficult period in my life, "God is enough!" And He is—for me and for you.

THE RESULT OF GRACE IN THE CHRISTIAN LIFE (VERSES 12:9–10; 4:7–10, 17–18)

There are two primary results of the grace of God when it flows into our life: We receive power and we receive perspective.

The Grace of God Produces Power *(Verses 12:9–10)*

Regarding his own situation, Paul said, "I will rather boast in my infirmities, that the power of Christ may rest upon me . . . . For when I am weak, then I am strong."

Paul states one of many paradoxes in the kingdom of God: I am strong when I am weak. He meant, of course, that when he was weak physically, God's power made him strong. And it took weakness on his part for power (grace) to be made manifest in his life. Paul was still going to be able to fulfill his calling as an apostle. It's just that people would see that the power in his life came from God, not from himself.

The little hints we have about Paul's personal life indicate that you probably wouldn't pick him out of a crowd as a great man who was going to change the world. Perhaps what was true of Paul applies to us, that the weaker we are in our humanity, the stronger God is through us. He could be "Exhibit A" for that truth, given what we know of him. If you feel weak in your humanity, rejoice! You are the very person through whom God wants to demonstrate His power.

A close friend called me recently to tell me of the trouble he was experiencing at that time. I was heartbroken to hear him describe what he was going through. But there was nothing I could do except promise him I'd be praying for him. I called him a few days later, and he had a glowing report: "Today has been a great day! I can't explain it except to say it's the grace of God."

That's exactly what it was. God's grace is able to cause things to happen that we can't explain. His grace is always sufficient and provides power to change situations in ways we couldn't have prayed for or anticipated. But we have to need His power in order to experience His power. If we are self-sufficient, then we don't need God. But when we are self-sufficient, that's when we are at our weakest.

I recall how broken I was during some of my cancer treatments. I was embarrassed that I could hardly preach and couldn't pray without crying. I didn't want to be weak as a pastor, but that's what God wanted me to experience. I needed to be broken of my self-sufficiency and learn to rely in new ways upon God's grace. And as that happened, I experienced a new sort of spiritual power that I wouldn't have had otherwise.

The Grace of God Provides Perspective
(Verses 4:17–18)

Yes, our afflictions hurt when we are going through them. But when we put them in proper perspective, they look different. Paul calls our afflictions "light" and "for a moment" compared to eternity. We are not to look "at the things which are seen, but at the things which are not seen" because they are eternal.

God doesn't instantly remove our pain because He wants us to keep earth and heaven in proper perspective. Life on this earth is not the real thing, heaven is. If we sail through this fallen world experiencing no pain, we'll get the idea that this is not such a bad place. Instead, we should be longing for heaven.

Here are four ways our afflictions help us maintain proper perspective in life:

1. Afflictions help us anticipate glory.

   Our affliction is light but our glory to come is heavy. If we can endure our light afflictions for a while, we'll enjoy glory forever.

2. Light things help us appreciate heavy things.

   When we endure troubles and afflictions in this life, they make us appreciate the glory to come.

3. Temporary things help us appropriate eternal things.

   When we go through hard times in this life, we learn to appropriate heavenly resources. We reach forward and grasp the grace that God has available for us which we never would do if we suffered no affliction.

4. Outward pain helps us accelerate inward progress.

As we go through trouble in this life, and especially as we grow older, our physical clay pot begins to wear down. It's a fact of life! But as that happens, we see our inner man making great strides in growth and maturity. We should work as hard as we can to maintain physical fitness so we can continue to serve the Lord. But the truth is, we're on a downhill slide until our body finally stops to function. But the weaker we get physically, the stronger we get spiritually. If we build up the inner man as we get older, we'll be far more able to manage the troubles that come with aging. There are limits to what we can do physically in this world, but there are no limits to what we can do spiritually.

The Grace of God Promotes Perseverance
(Verses 4:8–9)

Paul talks about perseverance in verses 8–9 when he says, "We are hard-pressed on every side, yet not crushed; we are perplexed, but not in despair; persecuted, but not forsaken; struck down, but not destroyed." We hang on through our troubles and learn to persevere.

There were four kinds of trouble Paul experienced, and four evidences that he persevered through each one:

1. He was pressured, but never defeated.

   The word "pressured" means to be crushed; so Paul says, "I'm being crushed, but I'm not crushed." He's feeling the pressure, but he's not giving in to it. He was put in prison, but wrote to the Philippians that the Gospel was flourishing. The more they squeezed Paul, the more good things came out of him.

2. He was perplexed, but never despairing.

   Being a Christian doesn't mean we always know the answers. Paul was perplexed at times, but he never fell into despair. If he didn't know what to do, or know an answer, he turned to God. Prayer is the answer to despair. You don't have to know everything—you just have to know the One who does.

3. He was persecuted, but never deserted.

   The word "persecuted" means to be pursued or chased. Paul was constantly being pursued by his enemies, but he was never forsaken by God. On occasion he had friends who deserted him, but he knew the Lord never would.

4. He was pounded, but never destroyed.

Literally, this last one means that Paul was knocked down, but he was never knocked out. Every Christian is going to get knocked down on occasion—but that's not a problem because we have One who will pick us up. I think it was A. B. Simpson who said, "The Christian life is simple. It's falling down and getting up, falling down and getting up, falling down and getting up, all the way to heaven." That was true for Paul, and it should be true for us as well.

The Grace of God Promotes Praise
(Verses 4:7, 10; 12:9)

Twice in 2 Corinthians 4 and once in 2 Corinthians 12, Paul uses the little word "that," which introduces a purpose clause. "That" means there are three purpose clauses in the three statements introduced by "that" in these passages. These three purposes reveal why God doesn't take all our troubles away. Here they are:

1. So that the power may be of God and not of us (2 Corinthians 4:7). God doesn't take all our troubles away, so we recognize Who really has the power in life to see us through.

2. So that the life of Jesus may be manifested in our mortal flesh (2 Corinthians 4:10). For the same reason that God was incarnate in Jesus, God allows us to go through trouble so the glory of Jesus can shine through us and the world can see Him. Like lights hidden under clay pots, God cracks and breaks the clay pots so the light of Jesus can be revealed.

3. So that the power of Christ may rest upon us (2 Corinthians 12:9). If we were never weak, there would be no need for the power of Christ to be near our life. But because we go through times of great weakness, the power of Christ can come upon us to save us.

In all three of these purpose statements, here's the obvious point: It's all about Jesus Christ, not us. Life is not about my problems or difficulties, it's about Jesus' ability to walk through them with me and give me grace to endure while I watch Him give me power to overcome—power I would never have realized without going through the difficult times. And the ultimate purpose and result of it all is that He might receive praise through my lips and my life.

John Newton knew this to be true. Newton's critics knew how much he loved his wife and predicted that, in spite of all his preaching about God's grace, he would fall apart the day his wife died. Well, the day she died, he preached at church and then visited parishioners the next day as was his custom. When it came time for her funeral, he preached the sermon in which he declared, "The Bank of England is too poor to compensate for such a loss as mine. . . . But the Lord, the all-sufficient God, speaks, and it is done. Let those who know him, and trust him, be of good courage. He can give them strength according to their day."

If you know Him and trust Him, be of good courage. He will give you strength in your day of need.

APPLICATION

1. Read 2 Corinthians 6:3–10.

   a. What is the connection between verse 3 and the rest of the passage about hardships? What do stumbling blocks and hardships have to do with one another?

   b. In verse 4, Paul commends himself as a "minister of God," then begins listing the hardships he had endured. Is the endurance of hardships an evidence of being a true minister of God? Does this apply to ordinary Christians, or only to ministers/apostles?

   c. What does patience reveal about a Christian? (verse 4)

   d. What does willingness to suffer tribulations reveal? (verse 4)

   e. Why would God allow His chief apostle to suffer needs? (verse 4)

f. What kind of distress do you think Paul suffered? (2 Corinthians 11:28)

g. Consider the experience of a single beating (verse 5). What immediate and long-term effect would this have had on Paul? (e.g., pain, immobility, infection) How much more would plural beatings have caused? (Note "stripes," plural)

h. What connection do you believe existed between Paul's personal encounter with Jesus and resulting commission, and his willingness to endure the hardships listed in verse 5?

i. Our commissioning by Jesus is indirect via the Great Commission (Matthew 28:18–20). Should we be prepared to endure the same hardships as those commissioned directly? Why or why not?

j. List the character and spiritual traits that commended Paul as a minister of God: (verses 6–7)

k. Which commends a minister or Christian more? Enduring hardship or manifesting love, truth, and other traits? How about manifesting those traits while enduring hardship?

l. Paul lists a series of opposites in verses 8–9: honored, dishonored; good report, evil report; unknown, well known, and others. Why did it seem not to matter to Paul which was happening—the positive or the negative?

m. How is Philippians 1:12–26 an example of rejoicing while at the same time being sorrowful? (verse 10)

n. With what did Paul "make many rich?" (verse 10; see 1 Corinthians 4:8; Ephesians 1:7; Philippians 4:19)

2. Read 2 Corinthians 11:16–29.

a. How many lashes had Paul received from the Jews? (verse 24)

b. Most of the things Paul describes in verses 24–29 we don't have specific records of in the New Testament. What is your estimate of how difficult Paul's life must really have been compared to what we read about in Acts?

c. Describe the hardships you have encountered in your life for the sake of Christ.

d. What did enduring those hardships add to your spiritual life?

e. How have other trials you endured as a Christian increased your appreciation for the grace of God?

DID YOU KNOW?

The New Testament is not explicit about the exact nature of Paul's "thorn in the flesh" (2 Corinthians 12:7). The most popular theory has been that it was some type of physical ailment or impediment given the reference to his flesh. Based on his statement in Galatians 4:15, some have thought Paul may have had failing eyesight. The fact that he dictated his letters and only added a personal greeting at the end rather than writing them himself also supports this view (1 Corinthians 16:21; Galatians 6:11; 2 Thessalonians 3:17). Others have suggested the thorn was spiritual, one of the false apostles in Corinth who, as a servant of Satan, masqueraded as a true apostle, attacking Paul (2 Corinthians 11:13–15; 12:7).

THE CONFIDENT PROMISE OF GRACE

Romans 8:28

In this lesson we learn that God's grace brings good out of every situation.

OUTLINE

We often hear people say, "Don't worry—everything will turn out for the best in the end!" That's optimistic, hopeful, and encouraging, but not necessarily true unless you're a Christian. God makes a specific promise to His children that everything works together for their good.

  I. This Is a Certain Promise

  II. This Is a Comprehensive Promise

  III. This Is a Cooperative Promise

  IV. This Is a Clear Promise

  V. This Is a Conditional Promise
    A. To Those Who Love God
    B. To Those Who Are Called

  VI. This Is a Conspicuous Promise
    A. Job
    B. Joseph

When I was a senior in college, God called me to the pastorate. Almost overnight I knew that God had changed the direction of my life. I didn't mind the new focus, but I was troubled by one aspect of it: I had been headed in another direction almost my entire life. I had been interested in radio from the time I was young. I used to build amateur radios and string antenna wire all over our house. And when I grew older, I got involved in radio production, working as a "dj" in college at an FM station. I then helped our college start its own Christian radio station. So I just assumed I would always be involved in some aspect of radio broadcasting as a career.

But I followed the Lord's leading and went to seminary after college to prepare for the pastorate. After four years of seminary, I did further graduate work and then accepted a call to start a new church in Indiana. About halfway through my time at that church, radio reappeared "out of the blue." I got a call from a local radio station asking if I'd like to host a live radio program. From that program grew another, and another, until finally, today, I am as involved in radio as I can possibly be. The program I host now is broadcast all over the world in several languages and can be heard in North America just about everywhere a radio is turned on.

So, God said "No" to radio only for a while. I laugh sometimes when I think of my original radio "vision" and what God eventually did. God had a better plan—He always does.

Sometimes it's difficult to see at the moment what God is doing in our lives. That was true for John Newton when he experienced a crisis in 1754. As he sat having tea with his wife before leaving to captain a ship on a journey to Africa, he suddenly crumpled to the floor unconscious. It was later determined he had had an epileptic seizure. He resigned as captain of the ship and never went to sea again. He later found out that the new captain of that ship was killed when the slaves on board revolted and took over the ship. John Newton's plans were changed, but his life was spared.

After this incident, Newton's wife, Mary, became ill. She hovered near death for nearly a year during which time Newton cared for her instead of working. When his money ran out, he took a job in Liverpool as a surveyor and reluctantly moved there, leaving Mary in the care of others. He believed he'd never see her alive again. Two months after settling in Liverpool, Mary made a miraculous recovery.

Through all these events, John Newton was learning that God's hand was always directing him, causing everything to work together for his good. God's providence was active in all areas of life, even the little things. His grace was sufficient to meet every need and to show how, eventually, all the pieces of life fit together.

In this lesson, we will study the verse that captures that truth more than any other in the Bible: Romans 8:28. Most Christians have relied on this verse as a bulwark when things happen they don't understand, an assurance that God is behind the scenes working all things out for our good.

We are going to look at the individual phrases of this verse to reveal how the grace of God works in God's plan and in our lives: "And we know that all things work together for good to those who love God, to those who are the called according to His purpose."

THIS IS A CERTAIN PROMISE

The opening words—"And we know"—convey a solid promise to the believer in Christ. It is an affirmation of the fact that faith comes by hearing the Word of God (Romans 10:17). We have to "know" the promises of God before we can feel encouraged, assured, or hopeful. Too many churches try to build up people's emotions, appealing directly to the heart. But the way to the heart is through the head. We have to know before we can feel.

When we are going through things we don't understand, it's important to remember what we do know and understand. Knowing the truth about God doesn't necessarily relieve our distress at the moment, but it does give us greater understanding and faith that He is at work. The phrase "we know" is used five times in Romans, and the verb "know" appears 13 times. So Paul puts great emphasis on what we can know for certain in spite of what we can't know.

For instance, in Romans 8:22 Paul says, "We know that the whole creation groans and labors with birth pangs together until now." That tells us that our personal groaning is only part of the groaning of the whole creation, that something better is coming.

On the other hand, "We do not know what we should pray for as we ought." So Paul is using an interesting contrast in this section of Romans 8. In verse 26, we don't know how to pray; but in verse 28, we know all things work together for good. We know the ultimate truths even when we don't know the immediate ones. Even when we don't know how to pray, we know that God is in control.

It's not unusual for people going through great stress to find themselves unable to pray. They're weary, they're stressed, they just don't know how to pray. They feel too weak to ask for strength. But even when that happens, we can know that God is at work for our good and for His glory. Someone put it this way: We are often the most certain about the ultimate when we are the most uncertain about the immediate! We need to be students of God's Word because what we don't know can never help us, but what we do know can.

Warning: Don't equate the truth of Romans 8:28 with a positive mental attitude or stiff upper lip. Sometimes people will say, "Just hang in there, brother, everything will turn out alright." That is an empty word because it is not based on anything more than a wish. If you want to know that someone is directing the affairs of the present for the good of the future, you have to know God as your Father. Romans 8:28 is a promise to the children of God (Romans 8:15–16).

THIS IS A COMPREHENSIVE PROMISE

Someone might ask, "What kinds of things does God cause to work together for good?" The answer is clear: "All things." There are no restrictions, conditions, or limits on what God involves Himself in for the good of His children. Nothing is left to chance. God incorporates even the negative, even the evil things in this life into His grand plans for us. Though death and grief are not good things, God can use them for good according to His purposes.

God does not prevent us being hurt or harmed in this life. That's not what the verse says. Things happen; then we have to decide how to respond. And Romans 8:28 says we can respond with confidence, knowing God is managing all the details in order to bring good out of the situation.

THIS IS A COOPERATIVE PROMISE

The words "work together" are the translation of the Greek word *sunergeo* from which we get our word "synergy." Synergy is the working together of various elements to produce an effect greater than, and sometimes different from, the sum of the individual elements.

When you combine two poisons, sodium and chloride, you get table salt. Separately, they are bad; but combined, they produce a non-poisonous substance. That's synergy. God is the One who can take a mix of unpleasant things and cause something good to come out of them—something different than any of the individual events; something good for our lives.

THIS IS A CLEAR PROMISE

God's goal in our lives is clear: "All things work together for good." His plan is not bad regardless of how things might seem at any given moment.

My eight-year-old grandson loves these new Lego-type building sets called Bionicles. They are a three-dimensional building toy with hundreds of tiny pieces that can be fastened together to produce amazing results. My wife bought a fourteen-hundred piece Bionicle set when we went on vacation so that our grandson would have it to work on when they came to visit. He dove into that box and began to work. But it wasn't too long before I heard him call to his grandmother, "Nanny, I can't figure this out. Can you help me?"

I was next to be recruited, and I worked with him for two and a half hours before throwing in the towel. I carefully boxed up what he had completed and sent it home with him so his dad could take it from there, but he couldn't figure it out either. Eventually, a ten-year-old neighbor figured it out. One piece had been installed incorrectly which set in motion a string of incorrect additions to the project. As a result, the whole building project came to a standstill because of the initial wrong move.

When solving puzzles in life, all we have are the pieces; but God has the instructions and the box top that shows the completed project. We can't see the whole thing, but He can. We have a piece that almost works, and we try to force it. It may work for a moment, but ultimately a lot of things have to be corrected because of that wrong move.

But God can take wrong moves that we make in our lives and cause the puzzle still to come out good in the end. That's the difference between Him and us, and why we need Him.

THIS IS A CONDITIONAL PROMISE

As I mentioned earlier, Romans 8:28 is not a promise that's the equivalent of the world saying, "Don't worry—it'll all work out." This is a conditional promise given for people who have met two conditions: They love God and have been called by God.

I'm not saying God never works behind the scenes in the life of an unbeliever. He is compassionate and merciful in ways we will likely never know about. But as a promise from a Father to His children, God gave Romans 8:28 through the apostle Paul to those who are followers of Christ—who have responded to the "upward call of God in Christ Jesus" (Philippians 3:14). His working all things together for good is part of the grace He extends to believers— the grace that saved us and continues to empower our lives.

To Those Who Love God

Simply put, those who love God are Christians; they are ones who are known by God: "But if anyone loves God, this one is known by Him" (1 Corinthians 8:3). "And this is eternal life, that they may know You, the only true God, and Jesus Christ whom You have sent" (John 17:3). To love God speaks of our relationship with Him.

To Those Who Are Called

To be called of God speaks of His relationship to us. When you say, "I love God," that is from your perspective on earth. But when God says, "He is one of the called according to My purpose," that speaks of God's perspective from heaven: "And immediately [Jesus] called them, and they left their father Zebedee in the boat with the hired servants, and went after him" (Mark 1:20).

So Romans 8:28 is for those whom God has "called according to His purpose" and who have responded to that call by loving Him.

The question every person has to ask is, "Have I met the two conditions in Romans 8:28?" In other words, "Am I a Christian?" If I am, then I can trust that God is looking at the box-top of my life, causing all the puzzle pieces to fit together for my good and His glory. One day, either on earth or in heaven, you're going to say, "So that's what that was about! I see now why God allowed that to happen."

THIS IS A CONSPICUOUS PROMISE

This is not theological theory we're talking about in this lesson. It is a promise that becomes conspicuous in the lives of those who belong to Christ. I've already given you an example from my own life as to how I realized, years after the fact, what God was doing when he closed the door on my going into radio. And you probably have concrete examples from your own life.

To conclude this lesson, I want to show you the outworking of this promise in the lives of two well-known Bible characters: Job and Joseph.

Job

Job, as you likely know, was an upright man who "feared God and shunned evil" (Job 1:1). He was very wealthy, owning thousands and thousands of head of livestock. They were all stolen by rustlers and thieves, his servants were killed along with his ten children who died when their house collapsed in a windstorm. He and his wife lost everything. Then Job was struck with disease. His friends believed all this had happened because Job had sinned, and his wife encouraged him to curse God and die.

But Job didn't curse God. In Job 23:10 we find these words: "But He knows the way that I take; when He has tested me, I shall come forth as gold." And at the end of the book, Job is resting in God. He knows God well enough by that time to have a Romans 8:28-type faith that God knew what He was doing when He allowed Job's tragedies to happen (Job 42:1–6).

Joseph

As you recall, Joseph's jealous brothers sold him as a slave to traders who took him to Egypt where he became a servant in the house of Potiphar. On trumped-up charges of improper conduct by Potiphar's wife, Joseph spent two years in prison. When he correctly interpreted the pharaoh's dream, however, he was released and installed as the prime minister of Egypt because of his wisdom.

During a time of famine in both Egypt and Canaan, Joseph's brothers came to Egypt hoping to buy food, never imagining their brother Joseph was the prime minister. By his wisdom, Joseph had prepared Egypt for the famine by storing up food, so he turned out to be the savior for his family. When the brothers recognized Joseph, they were shamed and feared for their lives. But Joseph spoke to them the Old Testament version of Romans 8:28: "But as for you, you meant evil against me; but God meant it for good, in order to bring it about as it is this day, to save many people alive" (Genesis 50:20).

Joseph thought his brothers had done something terrible to him when he was young. But it turned out to be what kept his family, and ultimately the nation of Israel, from disappearing due to the famine. For years Joseph lived with the confusion of what had happened, only to see the reason when his family came to him for help.

If you love God and are called according to His purpose, He is orchestrating the events of your life like He did Job's and Joseph's. Take your questions to Him and then wait for His answers to come in His time.

1. Read Psalm 139:16.

    a. What does David say was written down for him before it ever came to pass?

    b. What does this add to your understanding of God's ability to cause all things to work together for good?

    c. What does the phrase "fashioned for me" suggest about God's involvement in planning the events of your life?

    d. How does Romans 8:28 counsel against "panicking" when unforeseen circumstances arise?

    e. In light of the fact that God has ordained all your days, what are three responses you could have when an unforeseen event occurs?

2. Read Romans 8:28–39.

    a. What is behind the calling of God? You were called according to His _____. (verse 28)

    b. What is God's purpose for you? (verse 29)

c. List the five stages of God's carrying out His purpose in your life: (verse 30)

You were _____, then _____, then

_____, then _____.

d. What degree of certainty is introduced by Paul putting "glorified" in the past tense? (verse 30)

e. How would you answer Paul's questions in verse 31?

f. What is the evidence that God is serious about fulfilling His purpose in your life? What has He already committed? (verse 32)

g. Having already given the "best" that He has, list anything you think God would not be willing to commit to you to cause all things to work together for your good.

h. If God has justified you already, what sin could keep you from accomplishing God's purpose for you? (verse 33)

i. With Christ interceding for you, can Satan successfully accuse you before God? (verse 34)

j. How do the powerful final verses of this chapter relate back to verse 28? (verses 35–39)

k. How do verses 29–39 expand your understanding of WHY God would cause all things in your life to work together for good? What investment does He have in your future that He is committed to protecting?

3. List the issues you are facing in your life right now that are either disruptive, harmful, or tempt you to question God's protection in your life.

   a. Explain the difference between God making sure you "survive" these issues and Him actively using them for your good.

   b. How do you think each of these issues could contribute to His purpose for you of becoming conformed to the image of Christ? (Romans 8:29)

   c. What does it say about God if He failed to bring you through to the fulfilling of His purpose for you? How do you know that's not going to happen? (2 Timothy 2:13)

DID YOU KNOW?

The 300 years of the eighteenth, nineteenth, and twentieth centuries have come to be known as the Golden Age of Hymns. Some of the most prolific of the English hymn writers were Augustus Toplady (six hymns), William Cowper (68 hymns), John Newton (280 hymns, one of which was "Amazing Grace"), Philip Doddridge (400 hymns), and Isaac Watts (697 hymns). The most prolific of all hymn writers was Charles Wesley, who wrote 8,989 hymns.

THE COMPELLING PROSPECT OF GRACE

Titus 2:11–14

In this lesson we discover the past, present, and future impact of grace.

OUTLINE

We forget that our lives depend on oxygen until we are deprived of it. And so it is with grace. It is behind us, around us, and in front of us. The past, present, and future of the Christian life are all the result of, and dependent on, grace. It is the air we breathe as believers in Christ.

I. **God's Grace Has Been Revealed to Redeem Us From the Penalty of Sin—Past**

II. **God's Grace Has Been Revealed to Release Us From the Power of Sin—Present**
   A. Grace Teaches Us to Renounce Sin
   B. Grace Teaches Us to Rule Self
   C. Grace Teaches Us to Respect Others
   D. Grace Teaches Us to Reverence God
   E. Grace Teaches Us to Resist Laziness

III. **His Grace Has Been Revealed to Remove Us From the Presence of Sin—Future**

The phrase in John Newton's classic hymn that we use as a backdrop for this lesson is one that creates a power image: "When we've been there ten thousand years, bright shining as the sun . . . ." If you're wondering what that graphic image has to do with grace, be patient—it has everything, and more, to do with the glory of grace.

The verse containing this phrase is verse four, the verse in the modern version of "Amazing Grace" that John Newton didn't write. It was added, as I mentioned in a previous lesson, by a man named Edwin Othello in the nineteenth century. Interestingly, it is not wholly unlike a verse that John Newton did write which is not included in our modern version of his hymn:

The earth shall soon dissolve like snow,
The sun forbear to shine.
But God, who called me here below,
Will be forever mine.

This verse reflects what became a growing focus for John Newton as he neared the end of his life: His excitement about being with the Lord forever in heaven. He didn't want to retire, and he preached right up to the end of his life. He was far more excited about dying and going to heaven than he was about retiring. He remarked on one occasion that he was all packed and ready to go. He wasn't morbid in that sense—just excited! Would that we were all that excited about entering glory to be with our Savior.

Newton's preoccupation with eternity represents the final stage in every Christian's life. We have a past, a present, and a future. And in this lesson, we are going to study Titus 2:11–14 where all three stages of our life are mentioned. Paul begins this passage with the words, "For the grace of God that brings salvation has appeared." The appearance of grace is what sets in motion the three stages of grace that every Christian goes through.

"Appeared" is the word from which we get our word "epiphany." In the Greek language, it referred to the rising of the sun—there was an epiphany when darkness was overtaken completely by light. And Paul used the term to refer to the appearing of God's grace in Titus 2:11 and 3:4. When Jesus appeared, the grace of God entered the world and began to overcome the darkness.

John says that Jesus was "full of grace and truth" (John 1:14), and that, while the Law came through Moses, "grace and truth came through Jesus Christ" (verse 17). Mercy and grace appeared in the Old Testament on occasion (remember that David was not put to death for his sins of adultery and murder), but they arrived in full display with the advent of Jesus Christ. Grace "has appeared to all men" (Titus 2:11)—not all men receive it, but it has appeared to all.

Paul describes how the grace of God has worked to redeem us from the penalty of sin, release us from the power of sin, and remove us from the presence of sin.

God's Grace Has Been Revealed to Redeem Us From the Penalty of Sin—Past (Verse 14a)

Paul says that the grace that appeared in Jesus Christ was sufficient to "redeem us from every lawless deed." The only way to be redeemed from our sin is by grace: "For by grace you have been saved . . ." (Ephesians 2:8). Our good works can never undo our "lawless deeds" in order to qualify us for heaven. God doesn't grade on a curve, the good outweighing the bad. Only grace is sufficient to forgive us for those lawless deeds and redeem us from the penalty they earned.

If you are a Christian, when you were born again, the grace of God flooded your soul and cleansed your soul of the residue of sin. It was the gift of grace, not something we earned. Think of the blasphemy and sinful deeds of John Newton, the one who wrote about "amazing grace." He knew it was the grace of God that had cleansed his life from "every lawless deed."

Once we have been cleansed of sin, we no longer have to face the penalty of sin. God decreed through the prophet Ezekiel that "the soul who sins shall die" (18:4, 20). Paul said, "For the wages of sin is death" (Romans 6:23). But, because the grace of God appeared in Christ who died for us on the cross, we no longer have to die for our sins.

There are some times in life where we can look back and say, "I'm glad that's over"—final exams in school, driver's license road test, surgery. Now, just multiply the relief from those events by a billion or more and you should have the measure of relief appropriate by looking back at the cross and saying, "I'm glad that's over. I'm glad my sin has been dealt with."

God's Grace Has Been Revealed to Release Us From the Power of Sin—Present (Verses 12, 14b)

Yes, we were redeemed from the penalty of sin by Christ's death on the cross. But that doesn't mean we never deal with sin again. Our old sin nature was not removed at the cross. It is still there, vying with our new spiritual nature for control over our life. Fortunately, grace is sufficient to release us from the power of sin in the present.

The grace of God has appeared, "teaching us that, denying ungodliness and worldly lusts, we should live soberly, righteously, and godly in the present age . . . that He might . . . purify for Himself His own special people, zealous for good works." The focus of these verses is "the present age" in which we now live. The grace of God is our teacher, the Greek word being akin to *paidagogos*, or pedagogue, a teacher of children. The grace of God tutors us in how to live victoriously over sin.

In God's curriculum of grace, there are five key subjects.

Grace Teaches Us to Renounce Sin

In short, we are taught how to deny ungodliness and worldly lusts. The word "deny" was sometimes translated in Greek as "disown." It's as if we, when we became Christians, disowned the ungodly parts of our lives—denied them access to our hearts. I mentioned in a previous lesson how the Holy Spirit becomes our personal "Automatic Sin Alarm System," warning us when we are toying with something that could plunge us into sin and the resulting guilt and shame.

When you become a Christian, you become a brand new creation in which the old is passing away and everything is being made new (2 Corinthians 5:17). It is the grace of God that makes this transition possible. But it's not the grace we hear a lot about in our society today—the grace of acceptance, of toleration, of living my life, of just "getting along." No, this is the grace of the power to renounce sin in any and all its forms. When grace enters our life, we cannot tolerate sin in our heart; and finally we have the power to disown it.

Grace Teaches Us to Rule Self

Some have asked how the grace of God works in our life, and the best example I know is this true story. When the film, *The*

Passion of the Christ, came out, eight members of our church staff were able to attend an advance showing of the movie. The plan was to attend the movie, then on our return trip, to talk together about how to get our church members involved on seeing the movie and how to integrate it with some other things coming up on our church's calendar. Well, we attended the showing of the film; and all the way home, no one spoke. There was just silence. We couldn't pray, we couldn't discuss, we couldn't plan. We were just overwhelmed with the realization of what Christ went through to make God's grace available to us.

I remember thinking for days after that, "Lord God, don't ever let me do anything to wound Your heart. Don't ever let me do anything to bring shame upon Your name. Lord God, help me to live a life that in some way expresses my gratitude for what Jesus did for me."

That's what grace does. It so overwhelms us with the holiness of God and the price that was paid for our salvation that we are motivated to please the Lord—to live "soberly, righteously, and godly." To be sober-minded speaks of thinking clearly and carefully, to have a disciplined mind, to see things as they really are. To be a Christian in today's world, you have to be sober-minded. We don't live in a Christian culture. That means there are many conflicting ideas and worldviews coming at us every day. You've got to be thinking clearly to survive (Romans 12:3; 1 Thessalonians 5:6, 8; Titus 2:2; 1 Peter 1:13; 5:8).

Peter's warning to be sober in light of the presence of Satan is a serious warning. Satan wants to tear down your life, your church, your pastor, your marriage, and family—and the only way to keep that from happening is to live soberly, to be on the alert. We must keep ourselves out of situations where the devil is likely to be lying in wait for us. Clear-thinking Christians will always be thinking ten steps ahead in order to stay out of trouble.

Grace Teaches Us to Respect Others

Paul also says that the grace of God teaches us to live "righteously." This has to do with how we treat other people. Unfortunately, the church of Jesus Christ doesn't always do this so well. The number of church splits and fights through the centuries don't argue well for our appropriation of the grace of God to live righteously. The way we treat others is a mirror of how we treat Christ. The church is His body—if we don't act righteously toward the church, we're not acting righteously toward Christ.

Grace Teaches Us to Reverence God

Reverencing God means nothing more than living godly lives, to manifest God-like qualities and characteristics. We can agree on that. What is harder to define is how to become godly. Fortunately, the Bible gives us the answer to that question. If you are a Christian, you have everything you need, beginning with the Bible.

1. The lessons on godliness are available in God's Word (2 Peter 1:3–4).

   Peter says, "His divine power has given to us all things that pertain to life and godliness." Not most of the things, but all of the things. And how do we get these "things"? "Through the knowledge of Him who called us by glory and virtue, by which have been given to us exceedingly great and precious promises, that through these you may be partakers of the divine nature."

   We become godly by clinging to the great and precious promises in God's Word. The Bible is God's tool to make us godly. The Bible is what God has promised to bless and cause to spring up in our lives and bear godly fruit. The Bible is our manual on godliness.

2. The life of godliness is attained through hard work (1 Timothy 4:7–8).

   Don't get the mistaken idea that because godliness comes by grace that we don't have to work. The Bible doesn't teach that we're saved by good works, but that we're saved for good works (Ephesians 2:10). To become godly, we have to practice the disciplines of the spiritual life.

   Paul wrote to his young protégé, Timothy, to "exercise yourself toward godliness." The word "exercise" translates the Greek verb *gumnazo* from which we get our word "gymnasium." Lots of people go to a gym today to work out and tone their physical muscles. In the same sense, we have to work out to tone our spiritual muscles. Paul says that "bodily exercise profits a little, but godliness is profitable for all things." Staying physically fit is good, but it can't compare with staying spiritually fit. Paul says it helps in the "life that now is and . . . that which is to come."

Grace Teaches Us to Resist Laziness

The last thing Paul says is to be "zealous for good works" (Titus 2:14). This is a good word for Christians like us who are always teaching about grace. We say over and over that you can't be saved by good works—and you can't (Ephesians 2:8–9). But Ephesians 2:10 says we were saved for good works. It's possible to become lazy when focusing so intently on grace. There is kingdom work to be done in this world, and it is those who are saved by grace who are to do it.

In 1 Corinthians 15:10, Paul says he is what he is "by the grace of God." Yet, he says, "I labored more abundantly than they all, yet not I, but the grace of God which was with me." He is saying he was saved by grace, and it is that same grace in him that compels him to labor diligently for Christ.

So, grace redeemed us from the penalty of sin and is releasing us from the power of sin. That's the past and present. The future is that grace is going to remove us from the presence of sin forever.

HIS GRACE HAS BEEN REVEALED TO REMOVE US FROM THE PRESENCE OF SIN—FUTURE (VERSE 13)

The day is coming when we will be done with sin. All of the sin we deal with on earth—ours and everyone else's—will cease to be the nagging problem it is today. And that is what John Newton looked forward to, and what we should be looking forward to as well. Paul described that forward-looking attitude this way: "looking for the blessed hope and glorious appearing of our great God and Savior Jesus Christ."

I'm not sure how much of the church is living like Paul lived—looking for the return of Jesus. But that is the culmination of all the work of grace that has come before, the grand finale of the symphony of grace. There is not as much preaching on the return of Christ as there should be. It is the most relevant thing we could ever study. If you're a Christian, it's going to be relevant; and if you're not a Christian, it's going to be real relevant.

John Newton lived with two motivations in his life: the cross and the crown. The first coming of Jesus redeemed him, and the second coming was going to make him like Jesus. He lived looking back at the cross and forward to the return of Jesus. That's what the grace of God does in our life: saves us in the past and present and secures us for the future.

When John Newton died, he had already written his epitaph:

JOHN NEWTON

CLERK

Once an Infidel and Libertine,
a servant of slaves in Africa,
was, by the rich mercy of our Lord and Savior, JESUS CHRIST,
preserved, restored, pardoned,
and appointed to preach the faith,
he had long labored to destroy.
He ministered near 16 years as curate and vicar of Olney in Bucks
and 28 years as rector of these united parishes.

Neither in life nor in death could John Newton forget what God had done for him. His very last words were, "I am satisfied with the Lord's will." And he entered into the presence of His Lord.

APPLICATION

1. Read Romans 3:21–26.

   a. How (in whom) was the righteousness of God revealed apart from the law? (verse 21)

   b. How is that righteousness of God appropriated? (verse 22)

   c. What action is required on the part of the recipient of grace? (verse 22)

   d. Compare the use of "all" in verses 22 and 23. Why is grace available to all who believe?

   e. What is the cost to the sinner of being justified? (verse 24)

   f. In Whom is redemption found? (verse 24)

   g. Why did God require the shedding of Christ's blood? What was He demonstrating? (verse 25)

   h. Would God have been righteous if He had justified sinners without the payment of a price?

   i. How did the death of Christ make God both "just" and the "justifier" of the one who believes? (verse 26)

j. What was it about the sacrifice of Christ that made our redemption possible? (Ephesians 1:7; see also Acts 20:28; Hebrews 9:22)

k. When we are redeemed, what happens to our sins? (Colossians 1:14)

l. What three things did we receive when believing on Christ that we could never have attained on our own? (1 Corinthians 1:30)

m. What else do we receive at the moment we are redeemed? (Acts 2:38)

n. Were you redeemed in A.D. 33 or on the date you believed? Why is faith required to make the provision of redemption personal to each person?

2. Read Romans 5:15–6:1.

a. Count the number of times "grace" is mentioned in this passage?

b. What does that tell you about how important grace is to the whole transaction from death-to-sin to alive-to-righteousness? Where would we be without grace?

c. How much grace do you receive when believing in Christ? (verse 17)

d. Sin "abounded" in the human race. What did grace do? (verse 20)

e. Sin ruled before Christ. What does grace do now in Christ? (verse 21)

f. What is the answer to Paul's question in 6:1? Explain your "Yes" or "No."

3. Read Romans 6:1–10.

a. Why doesn't it make since for Christians to continue in sin? (verse 2)

b. What is Christian baptism a symbol of? (verse 3)

c. What are we able to walk in as a result of Christ's resurrection? (verse 4)

d. Why? (verse 5)

e. What was done away with in Christ's crucifixion? (verse 6)

f. If we died with Christ, from what were we freed?

g. If Christ is no longer subject to death, what are we no longer subject to? (verses 8–9)

h. In verse 10, "He died" is past tense, but "He lives" is present tense. What does that suggest to you about our ongoing freedom from sin in the present and future?

4. From what power of sin are you most grateful to have been released in Christ?

DID YOU KNOW?

In Titus 2:11–12 Paul says that the grace of God teaches us. We would be mistaken to think in terms of a teacher in the modern West, a lecturer. In the ancient world, a teacher was usually a live-in tutor who acted like a mentor to a child for many years. The teacher/tutor developed the child, which meant imparting infor-mation, encouraging, training, and correcting. This tutor was a *paidagogos*, a term Paul uses also in Galatians 3:24. There he says that the law was the tutor that led us to Christ. Once we come to know Christ however, grace takes over as our *paidagogos*, carrying us until we graduate to heaven.

THE CONTINUAL PRAISE OF GRACE

Selected Scriptures

*In this lesson we discover the place of gratitude
in one who has experienced the grace of God.*

OUTLINE

Keep a record for one week of every display of ingratitude you encounter—yours or anyone else's. The truth is, we are not nearly as grateful as we could and should be—and that includes Christians. Anyone touched by grace should reveal his gratitude in every word and deed.

I. **The Priority of Praise and Thanksgiving**

II. **The Perspective of Praise and Thanksgiving**

III. **The Possibility of Praise and Thanksgiving**

IV. **The Practice of Praise and Thanksgiving**
   A. Praise and Worship Every Morning and Every Night
   B. Praise and Worship at Midnight
   C. Praise and Worship at Meals
   D. Praise and Worship in Every Word and Deed

V. **The Perfection of Praise and Thanksgiving**

Abraham Lincoln once teasingly remarked that Harriet Beecher Stowe was responsible for starting the Civil War. She was the author of *Uncle Tom's Cabin*, published in 1852, that tells the story of a Christian slave named Tom who was sold to a brutal taskmaster named Simon Legree.

Tom had learned to read the Bible for himself, but Simon Legree tried to get him to deny his faith and live for the devil—just like John Newton had done to people he was around. Tom would always refuse, saying, "I'll hold on. The Lord may help me, or not help me; but I'll hold anyway and believe Him to the last." This only made Simon Legree more angry and determined to break Tom's spirit.

One night when Tom was feeling weak in faith because of Simon Legree's persecution, "Suddenly everything around him seemed to fade, and a vision arose before him of One crowned with thorns, buffeted, bleeding. Tom gazed in awe and wonder at the majestic patience of the face; the deep, pathetic eyes thrilled him to his inmost heart . . . when gradually the vision changed; the sharp thorns became rays of glory; and in splendor inconceivable, he saw that same face bending compassionately towards him and a voice said, 'He that overcometh shall sit down with me on my throne, even as I also overcame, and am set down with my Father on his throne.'"

As the vision faded and Tom awoke, "the solitude of the night rang with the triumphant words of a hymn, which he had sung often in happier days, but never with such feeling as now. At this point in the narrative, Tom's robust tenor voice sings verses five and six of 'Amazing Grace' [two of the three verses that have been left out of our hymnals], followed by the words of our last verse: 'When we've been there ten thousand years, bright shining as the sun, we've no less days to sing God's praise than when we first begun.'"

Tom gave up all hope of ever being free and focused his efforts on helping slaves know the hope he had for a future in heaven. Eventually, Simon Legree whipped Tom to death, having been unable to break his faith in the Lord.

We've learned in this series of lessons about the hymn that champions the amazing grace of God—the grace that gives us hope in our darkest hours. There is a great connection between grace and gratitude, for we remember what our lives were like before grace was revealed to us. Christians ought to be the most grateful people on earth since we have the most for which to be grateful. We owe a debt of gratitude to God for His grace that sought us out, opened our eyes, and saved us from our sins.

Paul was a grateful person. He constantly made reference in his writing to the grace of God and offered praise and thanksgiving for what God had done for him. We learn more about praise and thanksgiving from Paul than from any other source in the New Testament besides the Book of Revelation.

Paul even wrote to Timothy once that in the last days men would become "unthankful" (2 Timothy 3:2). I believe we can see that more and more today in our own culture. We should be the most thankful nation on earth, yet we seem to be the least thankful at times. There are even Internet websites set up now where people can go to lodge their complaints about anything and everything. There is even a complaint website for Christians! I can understand people who have never experienced the grace of God complaining. But Christians? People who've been given the free gift of forgiveness and eternal life, complaining? I'm not sure I understand that.

Our whole life should be a dress rehearsal for eternity. We ought to be practicing here the gratitude we are going to express to God forever.

THE PRIORITY OF PRAISE AND THANKSGIVING (1 THESSALONIANS 5:18)

The word "joy" occurs 181 times in the Bible, and "thanksgiving" occurs in its various forms 136 times. Joy and thanksgiving run like a golden thread through Scripture. In the Old Testament, giving thanks was so important that certain Israelites were assigned to give thanks before the Lord as part of the worship services (1 Chronicles 16:4; 2 Chronicles 31:2). I wonder what would happen if we had a Pastor of Gratitude on the staff of our churches whose full-time job was to remind members of the congregation of all they have to be thankful to God for.

Here are two things Paul says we should be thankful for: that God leads us in triumph in Christ (2 Corinthians 2:14) and that we have victory through Christ (1 Corinthians 15:57). Triumph and victory are good reasons to be thankful to God. I believe gratitude is a catalyst that puts into motion attitudes and actions that lead to victory in other areas of the spiritual life. I don't believe we can be fruitful if we are ungrateful.

Many people who agonize over finding the will of God for their lives are missing a very critical part of God's will: to be thankful. "In everything give thanks; for this is the will of God in Christ Jesus for you" (1 Thessalonians 5:18).

THE PERSPECTIVE OF PRAISE AND THANKSGIVING (1 SAMUEL 12:24)

First Samuel 12:24 has an interesting perspective on thanksgiving: "Only fear the Lord, and serve Him in truth with all your heart; for consider what great things He has done for you." We need to stop and take inventory on a regular basis and consider—remember, think about, meditate upon—the things God has done for us.

I read about some senior-age golfers who were filled with complaints as they walked the course. One of them said, "You know, these hills are getting steeper every year." Another one said, "You know, these fairways are getting longer every year." And a third golfer said, "These sand traps are bigger and deeper than any I have ever seen." Finally, after hearing all this negative stuff from his three buddies, the fourth golfer looked at them and said, "You guys just need to be thankful that you're on the top side of the grass!" There is much to be thankful for in each of our lives if we will just stop and consider the blessings of God. Remember the connection between thinking and thanking. Think and thank. When those two stay connected in our lives, we will be more grateful people.

Christian philosopher Dallas Willard wrote these beautiful words about perspective:

> He has never done anything greater for anyone, nor could He do anything greater for you, than bring you to Himself. Suppose He put ten million dollars into your bank account every morning for the rest of your life, but He didn't save you? Suppose He gave you the most beautiful body and face of anyone who ever lived, a body that never aged for a thousand years, but then at death He shut you out of Heaven and into hell for eternity? What has God ever given anyone that could compare with the salvation He has given to you as a believer? Do you see that there is nothing God could ever do *for* you or give *to* you greater than the gift of Himself.[1]

That quote makes me think of the lists of the wealthiest Americans we see occasionally. I wonder if those people have salvation in

Christ and which they would rather have if given the choice: their wealth or Christ? Regardless of how much money one has, God has already done more for us by giving us salvation in Christ than anything else we could imagine. And that is enough to make us eternally grateful.

THE POSSIBILITY OF PRAISE AND THANKSGIVING (EPHESIANS 5:20; COLOSSIANS 3:17)

Some people wonder if it is possible to live with an attitude of thanksgiving in everything as Paul says in Ephesians 5:20 and Colossians 3:17. People believe that their circumstances are the exception to the rule, that it would be impossible for anyone to be grateful in their circumstances.

We have to remember that most of Paul's admonitions about thanksgiving were written while he was in prison: Ephesians, Philippians, Colossians, and Philemon are Paul's "prison epistles," each of which mentions gratitude. So for Paul, gratitude wasn't situational. It wasn't dependent on where you were or what you had, but on your relationship with God. If Paul could remain grateful while in prison, I believe we can remain grateful in our circumstances.

Near the end of Romans 8, Paul mentions a series of events he had been through—tribulation, distress, persecution, famine, nakedness, peril, the sword—and declares that even in all those things "we are more than conquerors through Him who loved us" (Romans 8:37). We wonder if it's really possible to remain a "conqueror" with a grateful attitude in the midst of such circumstances, and Paul proves that it is.

THE PRACTICE OF PRAISE AND THANKSGIVING (HEBREWS 13:15)

Here is a little outline I have developed that reminds me of all the opportunities I have to express my gratitude to God.

Praise and Worship Every Morning and Every Night (Psalm 92:1–2)

The psalmist declares that "it is good to give thanks to the Lord, to declare [His] lovingkindness in the morning, and [His] faithfulness every night."

Our rising and retiring are like bookends on our day. They are perfect times to pause and thank God for His lovingkindness and His faithfulness. Beginning the day and ending the day with gratitude will go a long way toward keeping the middle part of the day filled with thankfulness as well.

Praise and Worship at Midnight (Psalm 119:62)

On other occasions, the psalmist rose in the middle of the night to give thanks to God: "At midnight I will rise to give thanks to You, because of Your righteous judgments." I don't know why David got up at midnight—perhaps it was to tend to the sheep when he was in the field. Not many of us have occasion to be awake in the middle of the night; but if we are, we can commune with God. The next time you wake up and can't get back to sleep, instead of tossing and turning, spend the time talking to God. You can at least thank Him that you woke up instead of the alternative! I have found that the occasional times when I awake during the night are wonderful opportunities to commune with the Lord in the silence of the night.

Praise and Worship at Meals (Romans 14:6)

"He who eats, eats to the Lord, for he gives God thanks." Besides sleeping, there is little we do as regularly as eating. So three times a day (at least), you can pause to give God thanks—and not just for the food you're eating, but for many other blessings as well. It's a blessing to be in a restaurant and see a family or small group of people at a table bow their heads and pray before their meal. It is a silent, powerful witness to others that God is in those peoples' lives and that they are grateful to Him for the provision of food and other blessings.

Praise and Worship in Every Word and Deed (Colossians 3:17)

This fourth category covers everything not covered by the first three: "And whatever you do in word or deed, do all in the name of the Lord Jesus, giving thanks to God the Father through Him." I can remember my first winter in San Diego, California, going to church on a warm, sunny Sunday morning, and just giving God thanks for the beautiful weather. (You have to remember that we came from Indiana where November is a bit different!) When you develop an attitude of gratitude, you will find yourself giving God thanks for many things you have taken for granted for years.

Praise and thanksgiving are excellent barometers for your spiritual health. If you are a grateful person, it's probably because you have experienced God's grace in your life. Like John Newton and the apostle Paul, there is a "before and after" story in your life that gives you good reason to be grateful forever.

THE PERFECTION OF PRAISE AND THANKSGIVING (PSALM 89:1)

This point brings us back to John Newton's hymn and the immortal words added to it from *Uncle Tom's Cabin*: "When we've been there ten thousand years, bright shining as the sun, we've no less days to sing God's praise than when we first begun." One day, praise and thanksgiving will be made perfect in the presence of God: "I will sing of the mercies of the Lord forever."

Since the days of their conversions, John Newton and the apostle Paul anticipated the experience of giving thanks to God in heaven. They were men of grace, which means men of gratitude and thanksgiving. The older they got, and the closer to heaven they got, the more grateful they became, and the more they anticipated being part of scenes such as that in Revelation 11:16–17: "And the twenty-four elders who sat before God on their thrones fell on their faces and worshipped God, saying:

"We give You thanks, O Lord God Almighty,
The One who is and who was and who is to come,
Because You have taken Your great power and reigned."

Besides the Book of Psalms in the Old Testament, there are more songs in the Book of Revelation than in any other book in the Bible. That says to me that heaven is going to be a place of rejoicing and thanksgiving and praise for all eternity. Our sometimes off-key voices on earth will become perfect in heaven. We'll sing together in perfect harmony with perfect pitch with perfect hearts. Those who are not living on earth as a dress rehearsal for heaven are going to be in for an awakening when they get there. There will be no grumpiness or complaining in heaven, so we might just as well begin living that way on earth.

Several years ago, something happened in the Washington, D.C., subway system that uniquely illustrates the effect gratitude can have as we manifest it in this world. The subway had stalled for no apparent reason; and the riders, eager to get to their destinations, were frustrated beyond words. They were complaining about anything and everything that had to do with making the trains run on time—the driver, the subway system, the federal government, the Washington, D.C., government. No one escaped their vitriol.

On the subway that day was a woman who had gone shopping and had purchased a bottle of perfume. She dropped one of her parcels, and the bottle of perfume broke. The scent of that perfume wafted up off the floor and filled the subway car she was in. Those who were there said later it was like a potion that seemed to defuse the negative environment in the train car. Everyone calmed down and began to talk pleasantly with each other until the subway began moving again.[2]

Such is the power of a grateful heart—one that has responded to the grace of God. "Therefore by Him let us continually offer the sacrifice of praise to God, that is, the fruit of our lips, giving thanks to His name" (Hebrews 13:15).

Notes:

1. Donald S. Whitney, *Spiritual Disciplines for the Christian L.I.F.E.* (Colorado Springs: NavPress), 113.

2. Ellen Vaughn, "The Underrated Spiritual Secret," *Christianity Today*, www.christianitytoday.com/ct/2005/011/26.46.html.

1. Read Leviticus 7:11–15.

    a. What category of sacrificial offering is being described here? (verse 11)

    b. For what purpose might a peace offering be made? (verse 12a)

    c. What was offered as a thanksgiving offering? (verse 12b)

2. Read Psalm 116:1–19.

    a. What does the psalmist promise to offer to God? (verse 17)

    b. He is thankful for something the Lord did. What was his situation? (verse 3)

    c. What did he do in light of his circumstances? (verse 4)

    d. What did God do in answer to his prayers? (verses 6–9)

    e. What rightful question did the psalmist raise for himself in verse 12?

    f. What decision did he make? (verse 17)

    g. To what prior commitment was he being faithful? (verse 14)

    h. What do you think was the content of the vow he made?

    i. Where were the peace offerings, or thanksgiving offerings, offered? (verse 19)

j. Why did he want to make his thanksgiving so public?

k. What advice did Solomon give about making vows? (Ecclesiastes 5:4–7)

3. What benefit do you see in public thanksgiving?

   a. How often have you publicly given thanks to God for something He has done in your life?

   b. What might an unwillingness to thank God publicly be a sign of?

   c. Scan Psalm 107 and note the likely reasons the psalmist recommended offering thanksgiving offerings to God. (verse 22)

   d. For what reason did the psalmist plan to fulfill his vows of thanksgiving to God in Psalm 56? (verses 12–13)

4. Read Nehemiah 12:27–47.

   a. What was the event being celebrated in Nehemiah's day? (verse 27)

   b. What were the Levites called to Jerusalem to do? (verse 27)

   c. What kinds of choirs did Nehemiah appoint? (verse 31)

   d. What did the choirs lead the people in doing? (verse 43)

   e. How official were the "thanksgiving singers" in David's day? (verse 46)

f. How were the singers supported? (verse 47)

g. What appears to have replaced official thanksgiving choirs in the New Testament? (Hebrews 13:15)

h. Instead of at appointed times, how often is thanksgiving to be offered in the New Testament?

i. How frequently do you find yourself giving thanks to God in an average week, outside of designated prayer times?

j. Why is praise and thanksgiving called the "sacrifice" of praise? (Jeremiah 33:11; Hebrews 13:15) Sacrifice implies cost. What cost is there in being grateful?

5. What are you most thankful for, besides your salvation?

a. How do you let God know of your gratitude?

b. In how many ways does gratitude to God overflow into gratitude toward other people?

DID YOU KNOW?

In 2003 two researchers published the results of their "Research Project on Gratitude and Thanksgiving." They concluded that gratitude was the forgotten factor in happiness. Those who kept daily, weekly, and monthly gratitude journals experienced many benefits: They got more exercise, had fewer physical problems, were more optimistic, achieved more personal goals, had more energy and enthusiasm, had more positive emotions and less stress and depression. They were more generous and helpful and placed less emphasis on material things. Their conclusion was that people who chose to be grateful and express their gratitude had a significantly higher quality of life. (http://psychology.ucdavis.edu/labs/Emmons)

ADDITIONAL RESOURCES
BY DR. DAVID JEREMIAH

The Authentic Christian Life

Many of the questions posed by the church at Corinth are the same as what Christians today are facing: relationships, lawsuits, divorce and remarriage, spiritual gifts, church discipline, how to read the Scriptures to get more insight. Paul's first letter to the Corinthians focuses on the inward and outward behavior of the Christian. In this three volume series, Dr. Jeremiah teaches us how to live as maturing believers and have *The Authentic Christian Life.*

Courage to Conquer

How did the Bible's greatest heroes confront life's challenges and conquer with courage? In *Courage to Conquer,* Dr. Jeremiah will introduce you to these heroes and share the source of their strength. When you discover the Source of their strength and make Him the strength of your life, you too can face life with the courage to conquer.

Captured by Grace

Captured by Grace is all about the multifaceted jewel of grace: the past, present, and future of the Christian experience. In this series, Dr. David Jeremiah reveals less-familiar aspects of grace, such as its plan, power, promise, and prospect—as well as the paradox of grace. If your Christian life is not what you know it could and should be, it may be lacking grace. Discover why grace is more than a blessing at mealtime. It is the source of every blessing you enjoy.

Knowing the God You Worship

Many of us know about God, but how many of us really know God as a Person? How can we expect to carry on a meaningful relationship with a God we do not know? This informative series will better acquaint you with the marvelous attributes of God. Once you know Him, you will realize how worthy the Lord is of our worship.

Each of these resources was created from a teaching series by Dr. David Jeremiah. Each series is available with correlating study guide and CD audio albums.

For pricing information and ordering, contact us at

P.O. Box 3838
San Diego, CA 92163
(800) 947-1993
www.DavidJeremiah.org

STAY CONNECTED
TO DR. DAVID JEREMIAH

Take advantage of two great ways to let Dr. David Jeremiah give you spiritual direction every day! Both are absolutely FREE

Turning Points **Magazine and Devotional**

Receive Dr. David Jeremiah's monthly magazine, *Turning Points* each month:

- Monthly Study Focus
- 48 pages of life-changing reading
- Relevant Articles
- Special Features
- Humor Section
- Family Section
- Daily devotional readings for each day of the month
- Bible study resource offers
- Live Event Schedule
- Radio & Television Information

Your Daily Turning Point E-Devotional

Start your day off right! Find words of inspiration and spiritual motivation waiting for you on your computer every morning! You can receive a daily e-devotion communication from David Jeremiah that will strengthen your walk with God and encourage you to live the authentic Christian life.

Sign up for these two free services by visiting us online at www.DavidJeremiah.org and clicking on DEVOTIONALS to sign up for your monthly copy of *Turning Points* and your Daily Turning Point.